# RADHAKRISHNAN'S PHILOSOPHY OF RELIGION

# RADHAKRISHNAN'S PHILOSOPHY OF RELIGION

PAITOON PATYAIYING

KALPAZ PUBLICATIONS
DELHI-110052

Radhakrishnan's Philosophy of Religion

Rs. 540



ISBN: 81-7835-643-0



Published in 2008 in India by

Kalpaz Publications

C-30, Satyavati Nagar, Delhi-110052

Ph: 9212729499

Email: kalpaz@hotmail.com

Lassertype Setting by: Dinesh Kumar

Printed at: Single Print Media, Delhi

# Contents

# MESSAGE

Dr. S. Radhakrishnan was one of the most distinguished and articulate philosophers of 20th Century. His scholarly commentaries on the Prasthana Treyi; The Upanishads; The Bhagavad-Gita and the Brahma Sutras-are classical works, which remain invaluable for scholars of Hinduism around the world. Personally, I looked upon Dr. Radhakrishnan as my intellectual Guru. He was always very kind to me and I learnt a great deal from him during our long associations for several years.

I am glad that a Thai scholar Dr. Paitoon Patyaiying has written on the religious philosophy of Dr. Radhakrishnan. From a look at the contents it is clear that he has done a great deal of work, and I am sure the book when published will be read with interest by all students of Indian Philosophy and admirers of Dr. Radhakrishnan's contributions around the world.

**- Dr. Karan Singh**

President, I.C.C.R. &
Chancellor,
Banaras Hindu University (India)

# MESSAGE

I am happy to learn that Prof. Dr. Paitoon Patyaiying of Thailand and an Indologist and Alumnus of Banaras Hindu University and Vishva Bharathi is engaged in the preparation of manuscript entitled 'Radhakrishnan's Philosophy of Religion'. Although I am not a scholar of Philosophy or Religion, I have studied Dr. Radhakrishnan's writings and tried to understand the philosophical moors. I send my best wishes to Dr. Paitoon Patyaiying for success in his endeavours. I am sure when the manuscript is ready the scholar working on Dr. Radhakrishnan or on religion or Philosophy will be greatly benefited.

**- B. B. Bhattacharya**
Vice-Chancellor
Jawaharlal Nehru University,
New Delhi (India)

# MESSAGE

I feel it to be a privilege to extend a message of my good wishes to carefully prepared academic work on Religious Philosophy of Dr. S. Radhakrishnan by Dr. Paitoon Patyaiying of Thailand.

Dr. S. Radhakrishnan was one of the greatest philosophers of the twentieth century around the world. His views on different aspects of Indian philosophy and religion and also on Western philosophy are great source of information for researchers in particular and readers in general.

I believe that after publication this work will be a welcome addition in the field of philosophy and religion.

**- P. J. Patel**
Former Vice-Chancellor
Sardar Patel University,
Vallabh Vidyanagar (India)

# FOREWORD

I feel immense pleasure to write a foreword to 'Radhakrishnan's Philosophy of Religion' by Dr. Paitoon Patyaiying.

S. Radhakrishnan holds a unique position amidst contemporary Indian philosophers. He not only did suggest a new method to Indian or Hindu philosophy but to the world philosophy of religion so that interested ones may comprehend the same to a great extent. He interpreted religion on the basis of philosophy and also clarified its meaning. Simultaneous to this, he put forward the significant views on most important aspects of philosophy-including God' and 'Soul'. These views will certainly inspire and guide the scholars, researchers and readers for centuries in many ways.

In the present work, Dr. Paitoon Patyaiying has largely served all those interested in the philosophy of Radhakrishnan, by putting therein, his immense labour. He has touched most of the aspects of Radhakrishnan's philosophy of religion. Along with this, he has, more or less, put before the readers many features of Vedic philosophy, known as Hinduism today.

I congratulate Dr. Paitoon Patyaiying for presenting such an important and interesting work and also wish success for the work.

**-Ravindra Kumar**
Former Vice-Chancellor
Meerut University, Meerut (India)

# INTRODUCTION

I always admire Sir Sarvepalli Radhakrishnan, the second President of the Republic of India, the world's largest democratic country and one of the greatest contemporary Indian philosophers. I consider him the real ideal philosopher king like Plato the Greek Philosopher, Lao Tzu, the founder of Taoism and Confucius, the founder of Confucianism in China.

He was one of the most intriguing philosophers who were deeply interested in religion at a time when there was also extensive agreement that religious belief, as traditionally understood, has markedly declined in its intrinsic significance for most members of modern societies. He uses the methods of philosophy to apply to world religion, which become philosophy of religion. Philosophy of Religion, according to his interpretation expresses the clear mark for the readers to understand.

This small book shows how Radhakrishnan reinterprets religion with his philosophical points of view regarding meaning of religion, essence of religion, personal experience of God, religious experience; its character and variety of expression, 'God' and 'Self', religion and symbolism, religion and science, faith and religion, intuition and religion. The book also presents his understanding of Hinduism for the readers to follow.

Indian philosophy offers to students at the Department of Philosophy and Religion, Prince of Songkhla University, Pattani Campus in both B.A. and M.A. courses viz.

| | | |
|---|---|---|
| B.A. courses | : 438-203 | Philosophy of Religion |
| | 437-205 | Indian Philosophy |
| | 437-311 | Philosophy in the Upanishads |
| M.A. course | : 437-502 | Basic Concepts in Philosophy |
| | 437-601 | A Critical Survey of Eastern Philosophy |

Therefore, Sir Sarvepalli Radhakrishnan's philosophy, including his examined study on world religions wherein he takes appropriate form within the religious traditions concerned, maintains an emphatic approach at the Department of Philosophy and Religion, Prince of Songkhla University.

It is my hope that this open-minded philosophy of S. Radhakrishnan which has dominated my thinking for most of my academic career will prove helpful to the readers. I would like to mention that by reading Radhakrishnan's Philosophy of Religion in the pluralistic religious situation of today, with its infinite religious experience; we ought to be able to escape from the small island of our own cultural tradition to the diversity of the deep, spiritual insights of different religious traditions. We will gain the meaningful world for our life and that world is perpetual universal peace through amalgamation of all basic concepts and features of all world religions, which this book represents.

I express my deep love and gratitude to my parents, Mr. Krob and Mrs. Bunchan Patyaiying, my mother-in-law, Mrs. Imchai Raksasri and my godmother, Acharya Poonpit Pitsatorn.

I acknowledge my indebtedness to Dr. Ravindra Kumar, Former Vice Chancellor, Meerut University who has not only taken keen interest in the present work but also has been kind enough to write its foreword. My sincere thanks are also due to my teacher, Assoc. Prof. Kampala Sirimuninda and to my colleague Dr. Uthai Eksaphang who took active interest in the publication of this work.

My grateful thanks are due to Mr. Sachin Bathla for making useful suggestions especially pertaining to the language of the manuscript, Mrs. Kamlesh Ravindra Kumar, Ms. Megha and Mr. Mrinal who helped me in preparation of it.

I am particularly indebted to my wife, Nisakorn, my children, Phil and Fame for their tireless efforts in supporting me in every matter.

**-Paitoon Patyaiying**

# Chapter I
# RELIGIOUS STUDIES - METHODOLOGY

## 1. Anthropological Method

Anthropological field studies since the 19th Century have replaced the speculative approach to the study of religion. They have brought to light, especially with regard to primitive cultures, tremendous amount of concrete facts about their culture and also about the modern societies. These datas have proved very helpful in working out the genesis of religious beliefs and customs.

E. B. Taylor (1832-1917) in his classic work Primitive Culture puts forward the thesis that animism is the point ofdeparture for the birth and development of religion. Fetishism and polytheism are only rungs in the ladder to monotheism. One of Tyler's contemporaries was John Lubboch (1834-1913) who attempted to explain the evolution of religion with archaeological and anthropological evidence. His revolutionary scheme narrates the growth of religion from the ancient to modern period as follows:

Atheism → Fetishism → Nature Worship → Totemism → Shamanism → Anthropomorphism → Monotheism → Ethical Monotheism

His book The Origin of Civilization and the Primitive Condition of Man proved to be a guidebook for later doctrines of evolutionism in anthropology.

But in due course evolutionistic explanation of religion met with severe opposition. Evolutionism is no longer an article of faith among the anthropologists. Thus the Scottish anthropologist Andrew Lang (1844-1912), for instance, discovered a kind of Urmonotheismus (primordial monotheism) among various primitive tribes on the ground that they also conceived of a High God as the creator and moral legislator of the Universe.

The anti-evolutionism of the Roman Catholic scholars is known as degradation theory. According to this theory, the most primitive man was in possession of a revolution of High God, but later this degraded itself into idol worship. This is in harmony with the Christian concept of the fall of man. The German ethnologist and Roman Catholic priest Wilhelm Schmidt (1868-1954) brought forward concrete evidence for a primitive monotheistic revelation from his study of various primitive societies in South America, Africa and Indian Ocean.

Many more recent anthropological studies have at least agreed upon the fact that the primitive religions are not mere 'stages' in the evolution of the 'higher' religions; they are themselves distinctive modes of knowledge and thinking. Paul

Radin (1883-1959) focused attention on the contributions of creative tribal thinkers to the formation of myths. Primitive religions have also scaled many heights of philosophical depth and logical precision. Thus Radin attempted to disentangle negative connotation from the notion of primitiveness.

The contemporary French anthropologist Claude Levi Strauss went a step further than Radin. He stressed more and more on the analogies between the primitive and sophisticated modes of thinking. He also devised a method of analyzing the myths. His highly acclaimed work ***The Savage Mind*** (1962) is concerned with the system of classification used by primitive peoples to organize the objects and events of their life. The latter's categorical systems are formulated in terms of symbolic structures. Myths and rites are those structures that utilize concrete images for conceptual abstractions. Levi-Strauss puts forward the highly controversial claim that these primitive myths and rites are as much rational and logical as the categories of modern science and culture. According to him the sacred objects are selected not on utilitarian grounds but owing to their suitability for analogical reasoning.

If Levi-Strauss is tenable then the notions of superiority and inferiority of religions are mere prejudices. But his critics have pointed out the intellectualistic orientation of his structuralism to the negligence of social and affective factors. Still his fundamental contention regarding the primitive religions as unique and sophisticated as per world-views holds ground with the recent anthropologists like Evans-Pritchard, Susanne K. Langer, etc.

## 2. The Sociological Method

The father of modern sociology Auguste Comte (1798-1857) advocated a three staged revolution of human thought in his ***Cours de philosophic positive***. Religion constitutes the childhood of man, metaphysics, the adolescence and science, the maturity. In the first stage nature is explained in terms of supernatural beings, in the second by abstract concepts and in the third by scientific causes. Comte emphasized the social dimension of religion. He argued that religious beliefs and rites bring about social solidarity. The elements of cognitivism and evolutionism are prominent in the ***Principles of Sociology*** of Herbert Spenser. He traces the evolution of religion from ancestor worship through polytheism to monotheism, but thinkers like William Dilthey emphasized the irreducibility of religion into any other categories. Instead of scientific explanation of religion, we should try for an inner understanding (Verstehen) of it. Karl Marx (1818-83) and his followers V. I. Lenin (1870-1924) and K. Kautaky (1854-1938) explain religion in terms of a social phenomenon: the class struggle. It is born out of alienation of workers from the products of their work and so from the society also. And it will end with the end of alienation in a communist society.

This and other forms of reductionism were opposed by the French sociologist Emile Durkneim (1858-1917). He considers religion as a distinctive aspect of social reality. By internally regulating the egocentric impulses of man, religion makes social life possible. Max Weber (1864-1920) was foremost among modem sociologists for his systematic investigations into various religious traditions. He also developed a set of categories like types of prophecy, the idea of charisma, etc. to deal with the comparison of these traditions. Another non-reductionism approach to religion is attempted by German bom American sociologist Joachim Wach in his book ***Sociology of Religion***. He emphasized on the practical aspect of religion more than on the intellectual, on religious experience than on the intellectual concepts and doctrines. Religious experience lives at the root of all forms of religious expression. All the beliefs, institutions and activities of religion embody some religious experience or other. Wach does not confine religious experience to a particular people or community. He is close to the Indian thinkers in his conception of religion as rooted in religious experience. He mentions that the ultimate source and the meaning of an expression or form valid in the realm of religion are its origin from and testimony to a significant religious experience.

Whenever such expressions are genuine, they are meant not to serve external aims and purposes but to formulate and perpetuate man's deepest experience, his communion with God. In as much as this communion can never be so completely consummated, its history must be viewed as a continuous process, lasting through what we call the history of religion, of which the history of groups created and maintained to foster this communion as a part. (Joachim Wach, 1947: 385)

Among the recent sociologists of religion, Peter Berger (1929), an American sociologist, has a place of prominence. He takes reverse direction from Wach. He attempted in his famous work ***The Sacred Canopy*** to explain religion in secular term. He calls his standpoint ***"methodological atheism"***. Another recent work in sociology of religion is J. Milton Tinners's ***Scientific Study of Religion***.

### 3. The Phenomenological Method

Phenomenological method involves two related things: a rigorous methodology and a philosophy developed in accordance with this methodology. Edmund Husserl (1859-1938) is the founder of phenomenology. He struggled for years to formulate the phenomenological method precisely enough so that philosophy-could be a rigorous science. Phenomenology has been further developed by Martin Heidegger, Jean-Paul Sartre, Maurice Merleau-Ponty, etc.

Religious thinkers like Rudolt Otto, Miercea Eliade, Gerardus Van der Leeuw, W. Brede Kristensen and Joachim Wach have applied the phenomenological method, partially and fully, to the phenomenon of religions. J. D. Bettis points out the following three differences between phenomenology of religion and philosophy of religion:

- Unlike philosophy of religion, it concerns itself with the full range of religious expression like the rituals, myths etc.;
- Instead of looking behind the culturally conditioned forms like philosophy of religion, it confines itself to the data, these very forms present; and
- Unlike philosophy of religion, phenomenology of religion attempts only to describe religious behaviour, not to explain it. Now what is the phenomenological method in relation to the phenomenology of Religion. Gerardus Van der Leeuw has characterized this method as follows:

  1. Assigning names to what is manifested (e.g. 'sacrifice');
  2. The interpolation of the phenomenon into our own lives, sympathy hectically;
  3. The application of ***epoch;***
  4. The clarification of what is observed by structural association (comparison and contrast);

5. The achievement through the foregoing of understanding;
6. Control and checking by philosophy, archaeology, etc.; and
7. The realization of objectivity or in other words letting the facts speaks for themselves. (Ninian Smart, 1973:53)

Rudolf Otto (1869-1937) applied this method to the idea of the Holy. Numinous experience lies at the heart of this idea. In this experience the other appears as the mysterious tremendum at fascinans or as a mystery that arouses both awe and fascination in man. This experience opens up a realm of reality which is holy. Still this experience is non-rational in character. In ***The Idea of the Holy*** Rudolf Otto says that the ***'numinous'*** is the universal element in religion.

But Geradus Van der Leeuw (1890-1950) considers power as the universal feature of religions. In his ***Religion in Essence and Manifestation*** he argues that religion constitutes man's response to his empirical environment through the concept of power. He contends that religion is free from anything supernatural or mystical. It only arouses the primordial experience of power in us.

The Norwegian phenomenologist of religion W. Brede Kristensen (1867-1953) the author of ***The Meaning of Religion*** and many other works attempts to organize the date of religion by using the phenomenological method without any attempt at their explanation. He discovered that religions could never be stripped off their historicity. Besides religious, knowledge requires an existential engagement in the object or knowledge. And this can be communicated only through symbols.

Mircea Eliade (1907) is influenced by Jung's analysis of myths. He is famous for his works on ***Yoga*** and on shamanism. He considers the distinction between the sacred and the profane as fundamental to religion. He also distinguishes between archaic and linear, historical religions. The archaic religion treats time in cyclic order. They teach us reverence obviously towards the Indian religions. Christianity is a linear, historic religion through and through.

Thus phenomenology of religion has provided us with description and analysis of religion ***sui generis***.

❖❖❖

## Chapter II

# RADHAKRISHNAN'S PHILOSOPHICAL DEVELOPMENT

Radhakrishnan is commonly acknowledged as the ablest and creative exponent of Hinduism in modern times and as a profound thinker of Philosophy of Religion.

His first work, ***'The Philosophy of Rabindranath Tagore'*** was published in 1918 which emphasized the ***Upanishadic*** elements in Tagore's thought. Right in this first work, Radhakrishnan shows his preference for Religion instead of the religious. But we find a radical turn in his outlook towards religion and his plea for the separation of philosophy from religion in his second work ***Reign of Religion in Contemporary Philosophy*** published in 1920. The first volume of his magnum opus Indian Philosophy appeared in 1924 and the second volume in 1927. In these, he ably interpreted Indian thought in the idiom of the west with an amazing range of scholarship. Despite his preference for ***Advaita Vedanta*** he did justice to other systems of Indian Philosophy.

In 1926 he delivered the lectures at Manchester College. These lectures were later published as ***The Hindu View of Life*** in 1927 and the doctrines of Hinduism in lucid manner. So this has remained one of his most popular books among the non-academic public. He delivered a series of lectures on comparative Religion at Manchester College, Oxford in 1929.

From these series of lectures, came out an ***East and West in Religion*** later in 1933. But in 1929 itself he delivered the series of Hubbert Lectures on ***an Idealist View of Life***. It was published in 1932 and turned out to be his most important work in the field of philosophy. It is a classic restatement of idealism which makes a case for intuition as a source of knowledge. His numerous later works may be considered to be the elaboration of the themes, discussed in An Idealist View of Life. Notable among these are the following: ***The Religion We Need*** (1923), ***Kalki*** or ***The Future of Civilization*** (1929), ***Eastern Religions and Western Thought*** (1939) and ***Religion and Society*** (1967).

### 1. Meaning of Religion

Radhakrishnan's attitude to the world religions is universal. For him, we are moving in the direction of religion, not religions. In Kamala Lectures he says that like the nation states, the great religions arose and developed in restricted areas of the world when intercourse with the rest of mankind was difficult. But now through the influence of science and technology, world culture is shaping itself. All religions are now attempting to express themselves in a new dimension and so are approximating to one another. Untenable doctrines are not so much refuted as set aside and the universal elements of religions on which there is agreement, are emphasized. This process will be speeding up in years to come and the gradual assimilation of religions will function as a world faith. (D. S. Sharma, 1944: 612)

With his great endeavour, he seeks to build a bridge between the traditional wisdom of the East and the new knowledge and rationality of the West. He is regarded as the Liaison officer between two civilizations. He tries to bring about a synthesis between Eastern and Western thought on the basis of spiritual experience. The spirit pervading missionary religion of whatever unacceptable to him. As Lawrence Hyde describes, the poverty of sectarian religions is like that each religion claims with absolute sincerity that it alone is the true light while others are will-o'-the wisps that blind us to the truth and lure us away from it. When it attempts to be a little more understanding, it affirms that the light of its religion is to that of others as the sun is to the stars, and the minor lights may be tolerated so long as they accept their position of subordination. (Lawrence Hyde, 1952: 371 - 372)

He defines religion as the discovery of essential worth and dignity of the individual; it is an invitation to spiritual adventure. When man starts remembering that he belongs to an order of reality higher than brute nature, he cannot be satisfied by worldly success or triumphs of material science. He then turns to religion which helps him to struggle with evil and sordidness and save him from greed, lust and hatred. It touches his conscience. It is not theology but special struggle for him to restore the lost relationship between the individual and the eternal, as the purpose of religion.

The aim of religion, says Radhakrishnan, is identification with the current of life and participation in its creative advance. It is a dynamic process, a renewed effort of the creative impulse working through exceptional individuals and seeking to uplift mankind to a new level. Meditation and worship are the means by which the mind, temper and attitude to life are refined. The object of meditation is the supreme Godhead.

For Buddhism, it is quite different as Radhakrishnan sees. Buddha is indifferent to the question of supreme personal God. For Buddha religion is to devote oneself with all one's thought and strength to the good life. It is a constant struggle with the forces of evil on which one has to rely on the strength of one's personality. By means of meditation one draws the power of the Universe into oneself and brings the soul into relation with the unseen. Buddha, as Radhakrishnan interprets, does not accept the view of personal God, since such a belief tended to indolence and hypocrisy.

It is the ethical interest that permeates for his attitude.

Again, he asserts, religion is the conquest of fear, the antidote to failure (Radhakrishnan, 1969: 96). The fear, which is an expression of man's rationality, cannot be removed by any change in his circumstances. It is not an instinctive fear which can be displaced by the stimulation of other instincts. True freedom from fear can be reached only by ***Jnana*** or wisdom; it is truth that casteth out fear. So long as religions themselves are an expression of fear, the security and protection they afford man, are purchased at a terrible price and end in distorting human life. The dogmas then lead to mutual destruction and the religious austerities become a trap for fruitless self-immolation. By demanding loyalty to warring creeds, which are arbitrary and unverifiable, men are turned against one another. The ideal elements of religions which make for universal religion and these beliefs and institutional practices which produce narrow group loyalties do not fit each other.

For him, religion is direct apprehension of the supreme Reality. (S. Radhakrishnan, 1967: 46) It is the attainment of a state of illumination. The Reality is omnipresent and therefore man is able to comprehend it directly within his own inmost being. Thus truth is enunciated in the Upanishadic maxim, ***tat tyam asi. That art Thou***.

He understands religion as a matter of direct experience. It is not awakening from a swoon, but a transformation of one's being. It is not in addition to one's intellectual furniture, but an exaltation of one's personality into the plane of the universal spirit. It is ***Brahmadarsana*** insight into reality, a direct awareness of the world of values. By religion, he does not mean any particular historical religion like Hinduism or Buddhism for he says that Religion does not mean merely ***Hindu*** religion but the religion which transcends, which changes one's very nature, which binds one indissoluble to the truth within and which ever purifies. It is the permanent element in human nature which counts no cost too great in order to find full expression and which leaves the soul utterly restless until it has found itself, known to its Maker, and appreciated the true correspondence between the Maker and itself. (S. Radhakrishnan. 1949:22)

According to Radhakrishnan in the various theories of religion, the inner being of man or soul is made into an object. All religions are human attempts to reach the Ultimate Reality. He gives an example from the great mystic philosopher, Nicholas of Cusa who categorically declared that ***"God is sought in various ways and called by various names in the various religions, that he has sent various prophets and teachers in various ages to various peoples."*** (Radhakrishnan, 1968: 59)

It is one of the tragic confusions of religious history', as Radhakrishnan sees, that when a faith becomes cradle, the creed by which man communes with the Divine supplants the Divine. The prophet who announces the message becomes himself an object of worship, supplanting the higher truth in which he believes. People then become accustomed to formulae, to prophets, and to organizations and turn them into objects of credulous faith and worship.

Religion from Radhakrishnan's point of view is an experience which affects our entire being, ends our disquiet and anguish, and the sense of aimlessness of our fragile and fugitive existence. This state may appear to be one of retreat, or escape from a threatening world. (Radhakrishnan, 1968: 58)

But in reality, it is a transforming experience that makes us aware of the Divine. It is spiritual consciousness. Belief and conduct, rites and ceremonies, dogmas and authorities are secondary and are significant to the extent they help oneself-discovery and communion with Divine. When the individual withdraws himself from all outward concerns, gathers himself together inwardly, and achieves concentration, there breaks upon him an experience, sacred, strange, wondrous, which quickens his inner spiritual life, lays hold on him and becomes his very being. Even those who advocate and follow science and reason have to accept the fact of spiritual experience which is positive. (S. Radhakrishnan, 1978:42)

Religion is a matter of experience; it is not a matter of mere dogmas or faiths; it is a kind of personal experience. If we do not have that, one may be truly religious even if one does not have religious experience. Man must be transformed, in that he has to become a different human being altogether as a result of his religious conversion. Without such spiritual conversion, man is not truly religious. Religion, he says, is not a thing which can be bought or got from visiting temple or churches or other places of worship. It is a thing which one can practice only by waging incessant war on the baser instincts which have so much command over human nature. (S. Radhakrishnan, 1978:75)

It is not mere contemplation of the truth but suffering for it. The human mind is crippled in its religious thinking by the belief that truth has been found, embodied, standardized and nothing remains for man to do but to reproduce feebly some precious features of an immutable perfection. Such a view of rationalistic self-sufficiency overlooks the quality of religions as spiritual adventure. According to the eastern religious traditions, the supreme fulfillment of man's life is an experience in which every aspect of his being is raised to its highest extent. Man passes then from darkness to light. (S. Radhakrishnan, 1967:427)

Religion is the self's discovery of its true nature or rather its recovery. It is the soul's dialogue with itself. Its secret is inwardness, self-security, inner cleansing, change of heart, renunciation, the unceasing attempt to create through love a new social order. Religion is not an escape from social struggle. Spiritual wisdom and social affairs must be brought into intimate relationship.

For Radhakrishnan religion is not to be confused with doctrinal conformity or ceremonial piety. It is the purification of the soul the remaining of self. It is not a mere quest for truth but a conquest of our selfishness, pride, greed, etc. It is through self-control that man can reach his goal. The extinction of the ego or its continual sacrifice is the way to fulfillment. Religion for him is not compatible with moral case; men cannot stand away from social life. We must love our neighbour in an effective sense. Though all men are born equal, we are not equal in many respects; we are equal in this that we are called upon to face suffering and endure it. We must, therefore, develop compassion. The path of spiritual growth leads one away from egoism, self-will, from a sense of personal superiority and leads him in the direction of humility, openness of mind, a sympathetic understanding in the needs of others and a willingness to take responsibility. (S. Radhakrishnan, 1968: 62)

Religion as a way of life is the seeking of the eternal. It is more behaviour than belief. If we believe in God we must act in the light of that faith. There are many who feel that outward conformity is all that is expected of them. We are said to be religious if we go through the round of ceremonies from baptism at birth to the solemn commitment of the body to the grave on death, even though this process is unaccompanied by any intense inward discipline or spiritual experience. If we repeat the phrases and make the gestures, we need not bother about the rest. Thus man of those who affirm belief in God or in future life act as if neither existed.

There is a difference between what we think, we believe and what we really believe. There is a story of the clergyman who asked the captain of a ship when a storm broke out what he was doing. The captain said: ***"We have done all we could and we can only trust in God."*** The clergyman replied; ***"Is it as bad as all that?"*** (S. Radhakrishnan, 1975: 60)

Religion should be an operative force in men's lives, private or public. It begins with an awareness that an individual life is not for him alone. There is another, greater life enfolding and sustaining all the individuals. Religion is man's search for this greater self, and true religion will not accept any creed as final or any law as perfect. It will be evolutionary, moving ever onward. In our normal experience certain events happen which indicate or reveal the existence of a spiritual world. The fact of the prayer or meditation, the impulse to seek and appeal to a power beyond our normal self, the moving sense of revelation which the sudden impact of beauty brings, the way in which our contacts with certain individuals bring meaning and coherence into our scattered lives, suggest that we are essentially spiritual.

To know one is to know all that man can know and all that he needs to know. A spiritual as distinct from a dogmatic view of life remains unaffected by the advance of science and criticism of history. Spirituality is the core of religion and its inward essence, and mysticism emphasizes this side of religion. (S. Radhakrishnan, 1975: 60)

Religion generally refers to something external, a system of sanctions and consolations, while spirituality points to the need for knowing and living in the highest self and raising life in all aspects. It is no use railing against God or destiny when we are ourselves the authors of our disgrace. If few are chosen, it is because few choose to be chosen. The Buddha laid stress on the creative freedom of man. The Buddha did not encourage dependence on the supernatural. He could not conceive of a being capable or creating a world for the express purpose of its creatures praising him. (S. Radhakrishnan, 1956: I-II)

In all religions, as Radhakrishnan points out, the life-affirming and life-denying impulses confront each other. Religion is not irrelevant to life. It has some guidance and help to offer to a generation which is perplexed at its failure to find satisfaction and groping for light. Only a living faith in God will enable men to overcome the paralyzing sense of despair and create a less imperfect society. Under the influence of science and technology which are becoming universal, religion is being transformed into a messianic materialism. Even those who do not adopt this creed do not feel the need for any religion. The vast unknown which held the mystery of God is gradually becoming the known. As our dependence on nature is diminishing, our need for faith is growing lesser. Besides, the infallible dogmas and doctrines fetter men's mind and the religious quest. (S. Radhakrishnan, 1970: 14 -15)

A truly religious man lives on the frontiers between the sacred and the secular, between religion and politics, between being and non-being. He is not called upon to get out of history and get into the desert and lead a life of renunciation and resignation. The saintly people participate in the work of the world and push it forward. Their every word is a prayer; their every deed a sacrifice. Men of saintliness belong to our religion. The question of attainment of the goal of life depends, in the last resort, on our spirit of earnestness. All life is great and leads to purity. Greatness lies in worthy living among the common things of life. In his opinion, religion will lose its redemptive power if saintly lives are not encouraged. No institutional patterns, no sophisticated theologies, can atone for inward spiritual poverty. The quality of our life is the evidence of our religion. The saints offer us the encouragement, not by their bearing blamelessness or effortless superiority but by the ease with which they face the risks and temptations of life. They make it easy for us to believe in goodness, though we do not take them seriously for we do not determine our conduct by their standards. (S. Radhakrishnan, 1967: 110)

All religions ask us to practice brotherly love. Love is inseparable from knowledge. Goodness and all encompassing care are the characteristic of Tao. (S. Radhakrishnan, 1967: 127) Every religion, according to Radhakrishnan, is based on a personal encounter, a human apprehension of the Divine, and all theologies are only attempts to translate the spiritual experience into words and draw out its implications. The majesty of God or the mystery of reality is so great that human language is inadequate to describe it. It is unutterable and incommunicable. (S. Radhakrishnan, 1967: 118)

Regarding the relation of religion to philosophy, he describes religion as a ***"disturbing factor in philosophy."*** ***"A religious system,"*** he says, ***"though the terminus of philosophies study should not be its governing influence. It does not argue well for the future of either religion or philosophy if religion becomes the starting point and dominating motive in philosophy."***

(V. S. Naravane, 1964: 234) He examines in this context, the view of Leinbntiz, William James, Bergson and Rudolf Euchen and shows that these thinkers reject monism primarily because of their theistic, religious inclinations. In none of Radhakrishnan's earlier or later works has the gulf between the religious and the philosophical attitudes been so strongly emphasized. In fact his effort has been to show that there is no fundamental opposition between the two. For Radhakrishnan, all forms of religion that have appeared on earth, originate from the fundamental need of the human heart. Man's longing for a power above him and greater than himself on which he can depend, and whom he can worship. The gods of the several tags of the ***Vedic*** religion are the reflections of the growing wants and needs, the mental groping and the heart-searching of man. Sometime he would want gods who would hear his sacrifices, and have god answering to this need. We have thus naturalistic gods and anthropomorphic gods, but none of them answered to the highest conception of the Divine, however much one might try to justify them by saying that they are the varying expressions of the Supreme One.

The scattered rays dispersed among the crowd of deities, are collected together on the intolerable splendour of the one nameless God who alone could satisfy the restless craving of the human heart and the sceptic mind.

The Vedic progress did not stop until it reached this Ultimate Reality. The growth of religious thought as embodied in the hymns may be brought out by the mention of the typical gods (S. Radhakrishnan, 1948: 27) viz:

1. **Dyaus:** indicative of the first stage of nature worship;
2. **Varuna:** the highly moral god of the later day;
3. **Indra:** the selfish god of the conquest and dominations;
4. **Prajapati:** the god monotheists; and
5. **Brahman:** the perfection of all these lower stages.

This progression is as much chronological as logical. Every religion, broadly speaking from Radhakrishnan's point of view, is passing through self-analysis and self-criticism and is developing into a form which is sympathetic to other religions. (S. Radhakrishnan, 1968: 68) No religion has yet uttered its last word. No religion can retreat from modernity and science. With the spread of scientific knowledge religions are becoming liberal, though a few cling to dogma as their only defence in this predicament. They are attempting to reach to what is of fundamental importance, that which is common and basic to all spiritual life from which each individual may gain a clear insight and a firm faith in his own religion.

According to Radhakrishnan, religion, if it is not to fade away, should undergo a radical transformation. (S. Radhakrishnan, 1982: 110) Ancient dogmas do not touch our hearts or satisfy our minds. Forms that were adapted to situations and issues that no longer exist are required to be changed. Our double beliefs have dimensions deeper than we realize.

Radhakrishnan makes it clear that if we do not interpret religion as a way of escape, we seek to make it a defence of the established order. All religions are conformist in spirit and try to appease those who hold power in the world. They even lean on them for support. The spirit of conformity and appeasement are not the monopoly of any one religion. There are some Hindus even today who are the defenders of caste and untouchability which are the offence and illegal today.

Christianity has no doubt been responsible for abolishing slavery and for righting many social wrongs, but as a community, the Christians do not profess to live up to the precepts of the Gospels. (K. M. Munshi and R. R. Diwakar, 1969: 96)

They do not see the beam in their own eyes, or take up the cross and drink the cup. The root meaning of the word "religion", says Radhakrishnan, suggests that it should be a binding force, and yet, by their claims to finality and absoluteness, the attitude of religion to one another is, unfortunately one of unmitigated hostility. (K. M. Munshi and R. R. Diwakar, 1969:100)

Radhakrishnan refers to the religious yearning of man, faction with the actual and yearnings for the Beyond are the keynote of all religions. Man struggles to attain perfection. Failure to achieve it, is no disgrace; to lack the desire for it is a misfortune. Man's struggle is for emancipation. Indian tradition believes that man has to grow from the intellectual to the spiritual level in the inmost recesses of his consciousness.

**2. The Essence of Religion**

Radhakrishnan holds that the essence of religion is not in the dogmas and creeds, in the rites and ceremonies which repel many of us, but in the deepest wisdom of the ages, the ***philosophis perennis*, *Sanatana Dharma*,** which is the only guide through the bewildering chaos of modern thought. The different religions, he says, are but the views or, apprehension of truth; they are varied historical expression of the Truth, which is universal and timeless in its validity. In support of his position, he cites St. Augustine's observation viz the Christian religion existed among the ancients but never did it exist, from the beginning of the human race until ***Christ came in the flesh***, at which time the true religion which already existed, began to be called Christianity. (S. Radhakrishnan, 1947:43)

He tries to show how the experience of the mysterious, is the fundamental character underlying all religions. He quotes Goethe who says: that

Man's highest happiness as a thinker is to have fathomed what can be fathomed, and to bow in reverence before the unfathomable. (S. Radhakrishnan, 1947:45)

For him, religion is rooted in a sense of wonder and eternal mystery, involved in trying to understand life itself, with its grace and power, or in the feeling of rapture when we reach the satisfying object; without these a man is as good as dead. For instance it is said in the ***Brhad-Aranyaka Upanishad*** (S. Radhakrishnan, 1947) to be pitied; on the other hand, whoever, having known the Imperishable, departs from this world is a Brahmin. Again, in the same Upanishad it is said: ***"If we know him here, then it is fruition of life; if we do not know him here that is the greatest calamity."***

Human life has no meaning if it is not inspired by a longing for contact with the eternal. Radhakrishnan describes not as a particular way of life but as the way of all life. Religious life is neither simply ascetic nor legalistic. It is not mere externalism and does not consist in obedience to laws and commands. According to Radhakrishnan, the world is an abyss of nothingness, if we take away its roots in the Divine. What the Hindu thinkers aim at, is action without attachment. The action of an individual who is no more a victim of selfishness, who has identified himself with the divine centre which is in him and in all things is no action in the ordinary sense. Since he is not emotionally involved in the fruits of action, he is able to act effectively. Thus pure religion is withdrawal from the world and also returns to it. Its aim is the control of life by the power of spirit. The spirit of religion is that man must effect the change within his own nature in order to let the divine in him manifest it fully. It speaks of death of man as we know him, with all worldly desires, and the emergence of a new man, a man spiritually awakened and fulfilled. This is the teaching not only of the ***Upanishads*** and Buddhism but also of the Greek mysteries and Platonist, of Gospels and the schools of Gnosticism. (Paul Arthur Schilpp, 1962:80)

***"Religion",*** Radhakrishnan states, ***"is native to the human mind, integral to human nature itself. Everything also may dissolve, but belief in God, which is the ultimate confession of all the faiths of the world, remains."*** (Paul Arthur Schilpp, 1962: 419)

He tries to use his interpretation to tell us that religion emphasizes mainly the following:

***Abhaya***, or freedom from fear, is a temper of mind, but not the acceptance of a belief or the practice of a rite. Because of it, our fellow-men are seen as something more than mere creatures of time and place separated from us by the accidents of nature and set against us by the necessities of animal existence. The real state of ***Abhaya*** is attained when the same self is seen in all. Then there remains nothing to be afraid of. It is to apprehend the reality of other souls. The law of love is then obeyed not because of its being our religious duty but because life which has been more fully revealed, consists in loving.

***Ahimsa*** or fellow-feeling for all living things, which include in its merciful arms, even the lowest forms of animal life, is the natural fruit of ***Abhaya***. The marks of genuine religion are ***Abhaya*** or freedom from fear, expressing itself in harmony, balance, perfect agreement between body and soul, between the hands and the brain, and ***Ahimsa*** or love, ***Abhaya*** and ***Ahimsa***, awareness and sympathy, freedom and love, are the two characteristics, theoretical and practical, of religion.

According to Radhakrishnan, the soul in its solitude is the birthplace of religion. (K. M. Munshi and R. R. Diwakar, 1969: 162) Moses on the lonely Mount of Sinai, Buddha under the Bodhi Tree were lost in contemplation, and Jesus by_the Jordan in the stillness or prayer, Paul in the lonely sojourn in the desert, Mohammad on a solitary mount at Mecca, Francis of Assisi in his prayers in the remote crags of the highland of Alverno, found the strength and the assurance of the Reality of God. Everything that is great, new and creative in religion rises out of the unfathomable depths of the soul, in the quiet of prayer, and in the solitude of meditation.

Religion is a strenuous endeavour to

apprehend truth (K. M. Munshi and R. R. Diwakar, 1969: 430) Dogmas and rites are intended to awaken in us the spiritual sense and to help us to realise new possibilities of our existence. Religious forms without religious experience do not satisfy man's longing for spiritual fulfillment. True religion means whole-hearted commitment and dedication, in moments of devotion and prayer; we offer our whole being to an integral reality without claiming any reward for ourselves. Religious experience unites rather than divides in it the sense of separateness is transcended.

We have today not a confrontation of religion but a meeting of them; it would have been a betrayal of one's faith to seek to find what is valuable in other religions, in the last century. There are representative leaders of different living faith, pledge to mutual understanding. They stress the common aim of religions and not the things, which separate them. No religion today encourages mere revival or repetition of the past. All religions stress the common inheritance and plead for progress along a path of mutual respect and understanding. We feel that we are all partners in the same quest.

Radhakrishnan seems sure that the meeting together of the religions has contributed to the vitality of these religions. (S. Radhakrishnan, 1967: 128) Religious isolationism is no longer possible. It is today one of the possibilities of a student of religion to understand the existence of other religions, each with its own claims. The different religious traditions are governed by the same spirit, and work for the redemption of both man and the universe. Cosmic salvation is the aim of all religions.

According to Radhakrishnan, a study of other religions is essential for the understanding of one's own and is a valuable constituent of one's general culture. (S. Radhakrishnan, 1967: 134) It is true that no one can master all the scriptures of the world. We must work for a new spiritual reconciliation and outlook in the light of recent developments with the aim of living together in harmony. The great prophets reveal to us the new being.

Radhakrishnan also believes that the true religion, however, agrees with the social idealists in affirming that life eternal is to be realized on this earth itself. Love of man is as fundamental to religion as worship of God. We must seek our evolution through the medium of life, by transforming it, by changing it over. Some social idealists believe that the opposition of two world orders is the essence of all religions. But this is not true. Faced by the sorrow and suffering of the world, Buddha endeavourered to banish them. He did not ignore or explain them away, but as a profound revolutionary tries to overcome them. This is one of the concrete evidences among many to establish the social utility of religion.

But when Professor Whitehead defines religion

as ***"What the individual does with his own solitariness,"*** (S. Radhakrishnan, 1967: 104).

Radhakrishnan tells us that the former is stressing upon the fact that it is not a mere social phenomenon. It is not an apologetic for the existing social order; nor is it a mere instrument for social salvation. It is an attempt to discover the ideal possibilities of human life, a quest for emancipation of individual too.

### 3. Personal experience of God

Radhakrishnan points out that most of the religions owe their inspiration to the personal insights of their prophet founders. (S. Radhakrishnan, 1971: 70) But the Hindu religion, for example, is characterized by its adherence to religious experiences of a succession of seers, in its pure form, at any rate; it never leaned as heavily as other religions on authority. It is not a ***"founded"*** religion; nor does its centre found any historical events. Its distinctive characteristic has been its insistence on the inward life of spirit. To know, possess and be the spirit in the physical frame to discover and realize the life divine in a body subject to sickness and death has been the constant aim of the ***Hindu*** religious endeavour.

The ***Hindu*** looks back to the ***Vedic*** period and the epoch of their founders. The wisdom of the ***Vedas*** is accepted name for the highest spiritual truth of which the human mind is capable. It is the

Work of the ***Rishis*** or the seers. The insight of the ***Rishis*** is not evolved as the result of logical reasoning or systematic philosophy but is the products of spiritual intuition, ***'Drishti'*** or vision. The ***Rishis*** are not so much the authors of the truths recorded in the ***Vedas***, one are the seers who were able to discern the eternal truths by raising their life-spirit to the plane of the universal spirit. They are the pioneer researchers in the realm of spirit who saw more in the world than their fellow human beings. Their utterances are based not on transitory vision but on a continuous experience of resident life and power. When the ***Vedas*** are regarded as the highest authority, all that meant is that the most exacting of all authorities is the authority of facts.

Radhakrishnan thinks that if experience is the soul of religion, expression is the body through which it fulfils its destiny. We have the spiritual facts and their interpretation by which they are communicated to others.

***Shankara*** describes them as ***Pratvaksa*** or direct knowledge in the soul and expressions which are indirect. Intuitions abide, while interpretation change. (S. Radhakrishnan, 1971: 71)

***Shruti*** and ***Smriti*** differ as the authority of fact and the authority of interpretation. Theory, speculation, and dogmas change from time to time as the facts become better understood. Their value is acquired from their adequacy to experience. When forms dissolve and the interpretations are doubted, it is a call to get back to the experience itself and reformulate its content in more suitable terms. While the experimental character of religion is emphasized in the Hindu faith, every other religion at it best, falls back on it. The whole schemes of Buddhism centers around Buddha's enlightenment. Moses saw God in the burning bush, and ***Elijah*** heard small voice, in ***Jeramiah*** we read that this is the covenant which I will make with the house of Israel after those days, said the Lord. I will put my hand in their inward parts, and in their heart I will write it. Jesus' experience of God is the basic fact for Christianity, ***"As he came up out of the river he saw the heavens part above him and the spirit descending like a dove towards him; and he heard a voice sounding out of the heavens and saying, 'Thou art my beloved son. I have chosen thee'."***

But as a matter of fact, Radhakrishnan says, religion cannot escape from symbolism, from incense and crucifixes, from rites and dogmas. (S. Radhakrishnan, 1949: 89)

Those forms are employed by religion to focus its faith, but when they become more important than the faith itself, we have idolatry. A symbol does not subject the infinite to the finite, but renders the finite transparent. It aids us to see the infinite through it. When, however, we confuse the symbol with the reality, exalt the relative to the status of the Absolute, difficulties arise and an unjustified idolatry develops. It is this type of idolatry that stands in the way of religious fellowship and understanding.

Every dogmatic religion overlooks the spiritual facts, and worship theological opinions. It is more anxious for the spread of its dogmas than for the spiritual education of human race. If we realize the true place of symbolism, then we shall not bother about how men reach the knowledge of spiritual reality. The different religious groups bound themselves by means of rites and ceremonies stand against the formation of a human society. Intuitive religion rebels against these communal and national gods, confident in the one spirit whose presence informs and illumines the whole of mankind. Religion, as Radhakrishnan sees it, speaks to us in many dialectics. It has diverse complexions. And yet it has one true voice, the voice of human piety and compassion, of mercy, of patient love, and to that voice we must do all we can to listen. Naturally, a sensitive soul is bound to be outraged by the social order which is at the end of one age and the beginning of another. (S. Radhakrishnan, 1947: 100) Radhakrishnan summarizes that the central dogma of true religion is the possible perfection of man, his inherent divinity, and the invisible solidarity of all living beings with each other in the life of God. (S. Radhakrishnan, 1929: 68) Again on the object of religion he says that it is an ideal in contrast to the present state. (S Radhakrishnan, 1949: 42 - 43) ***Dharma*** is the unity of all deal ends, arousing us to desire and action. It controls us because of its inherent meaning and value, and not because it is already in a realized existence apart from us. The reality of ***Dharma*** is vouched for by its undeniable power of action. The Buddha insists that it is not wholly without roots in existence. He objects to any identification of dharma with a being outside nature. To imagine that dharma or the ideal of morality is external to nature is to imply that the natural means are corrupt and unimportant. It is to make out that fundamentally man is evil, and regeneration is a matter of grace. The improvement of human character is then regarded not as the natural result of human effort, but as a sudden and complete transmutation achieved through the aid of the supernatural. But for the Buddha the impulse to dharma, to justice and kindliness is operative in things, and its efficient activity will mean the reduction of disorder, cruelty and oppression. ***Dharma*** is organic to existence.

Radhakrishnan believes that the true religion consists in an insight into the first principle of God or in personal knowledge of Him, not merely in dogmatic statements about Him. It is seeing Him face to face and that constitutes the essential basis of religion. (S. Radhakrishnan, 1978: 44) When Swami Vivekananda asked Sri Ramakrishna, ***"Have you seen God?" "Yes, I have seen him more clearly and intensely than I see you."*** This shows that a direct vision of God is the soul of religion.

Similarly, it is said in the ***Rig-Veda*** viz ***tad visnoh paramam padam sada pasyanti surayah divism caksurtatam***. (S. Radhakrishnan, 1978: 45).

The word used here is ***nanvanti***; the sages see constantly the highest dwelling place of divine, even as our eyes see the riot of colour spread out before us in the skies. Even as the eyes see the sky, so does the soul of man apprehend God. So it is the personal encounter with or personal insight into the nature of Supreme that constitutes the essence of religion.

Radhakrishnan points to the ***Upanishad*** to say that what we ought to have is a direct knowledge of God, an illumined personal experience of the Supreme but not an intellectual understanding. There is a world of difference between those who say ***Asti Brahma*** and those who say ***Aham Brahmeasmi***. (S. Radhakrishnan, 1978: 45) There are people who go about saying God exists, but such knowledge of the existence of God is indirect; it is not personal, it is merely theoretical and borrowed knowledge. The end of religion, therefore, in a personal encounter with the Divine. It is a personal insight into the ultimate root of things. This is what constitutes the real religious life of man.

The personal encounter with God, or direct experience of God, according to Radhakrishnan, cannot be adequately expressed logically and verbally. Our words along with the mind return baffled; unable to comprehend that personal experience. Such experience is what we feel, but cannot express by means of words or by means of logical propositions. Every form in an approximation; shadow of that ultimate substance. It is a substance which we have to realize and recognize; after that all the words which we use resemblances or shadows or approximations. That is why the ***Rig-Veda*** says, ***okam sad vipra vadanti***. (S. Radhakrishnan, 1978: 47) the real is one but people speak of it in various ways. So also the Upanishad says that ***'hrda manisa manasa adhiklinte***[1]. We fabricate by our intelligence, by our mind. By the words, we try to express the inexpressible. God is immense. He refuses to be caught in our categories. Therefore we refuse to say that there is any particular denomination or any particular expression of the Supreme Reality.

When we recognize that religion is personal experience of the Divine and later recognize that all - expressions are faulty, fallible, fragmentary expressions of that one Supreme reality, we can't put up with religious bigotry and human misery that happen in this world. We have to apply ourselves for their removal. We have to participate in the agony of this world. We have to crucify ourselves until we are able to restore the truth to all human beings, until humanity is redeemed, so to say, until religions redeem themselves from their evil past.

The greatest of the religious seekers, the

greatest of religious seers, therefore went out, casting aside all their possessions, throwing themselves into the whirlpool of this world to raise its status to a higher level. Service of man is the ultimate expression of any kind of religion. If we realize, therefore, that religion is insight into reality, and that there are many ways in which religious truth can be expressed and the test of a religion is not belief but deed. Then we have grasped the essence of all religions; that is what Ramakrishna, Vivekananda and every great seer of this world has said.

It is very important, Radhakrishnan says, to get rid of religious antagonism, and animosities which separate man from man; and hence make them get back to the roots of reality and make them understand what true religion is. It is because we are religious with our spinal cord, not with our whole being, that we have all religious divisions. The religious differences should not make any difference to the treatment which we give to human beings, because they constitute one single family. Based on the oneness of the spirit, humanity must be recognized as one family. If we do that, then we are truly religious but not when we harbour greed, passion, love of power, love of putting down the other man.

A truly religious man must bring about an inward transformation of his being and must rid himself of any kind of greed, anger, hatred, etc., and must look upon the whole world as his kindred (S. Radhakrishnan, 1978: 52) He is a religious man who has rid himself of passion and has become truly dispassionate. According to Radhakrishnan, it does not matter what religion we profess. All religions insist on the same kind of intense self-discipline. The moral crisis of the world today is the direct result of divorces between theory and practice.

## 4. Religious Experience

Religious Experience, Radhakrishnan says, is as old as our smiling and weeping, loving and forgiving, the sense of God is induced within us in several ways, through communion with nature, through worship of goodness even through natural events like sunset and death. (S. Radhakrishnan, 1947:42)

It ranges all the way from the gentle heightening of life to the intense degree of ecstasy in God.

Radhakrishnan believes that when rational thought is applied to the empirical data of the world and of the human self, the conclusion of a Supreme who is Pure Being and Free Activity is reached (Paul Arthur Schilpp, 1962: 60) but it can be argued that it is only a necessity of thought, a hypothesis, however valid it may be. But still there is also an ancient and widespread tradition that we can apprehend Eternal Being with the directness and immediacy. When ***Upanishad*** speaks of ***Janna*** of gnosis, when Buddha speaks of Bodhi of enlightenment, when Jesus speaks of the truth that will make us free, ***"they refer to the direct spiritual apprehension of the Supreme, in which the gap between truth and Being is closed."*** Thus to them religion rests on the testimony of the Holy Spirit, on personal experience, on mysticism or ***cognitio dei experimentalis*** as defined by St. Thomas Aquinas. From the affirmation of spiritual experience, it is possible to reconcile the conclusions of logical understanding with the apprehensions of integral insight.

Radhakrishnan thinks that there is a tradition of direct apprehension of the Supreme in all lands, in all ages and in all creeds. The seers describe their experience with an impressive unanimity. Indian religions, he says, take their stand on spiritual experience, on divine-human encounter, ***Krishnariunasamvada***, and so do the prophets and saints of other religions. Augustine writes that I entered and beheld with the eye of my soul above the same eye of my soul, above my mind, the Light unchangeable.

Acording to Radhakrishnan, St. Bernard says that Happy and blessed is he ***"who once or twice or even once only-in this mortal life for the space of a moment, has lost himself in god"***. (Paul Arthur Schilpp, 1962: 58)

For him the word "Awake" whom the ***Upanishads***, the Buddha and Jesus use means ***"experience."***

It is not an awakening from a swoon, but a transformation of one's being. (S. Radhakrishnan, 1949: 71) It is not an addition to one's intellectual furniture, but an exaltation of one's personality into the plane of the universal spirit. It is ***Brahmadarsana***-insight into reality, a direct awareness of the world of values. Religious experience is not to be confused with the pursuit of truth, beauty or goodness. It is a life of adoring love, transcending these. Religious experience, when genuine, is characterized by vividness, directness, freshness and joy. In it we feel the impact of Reality. It is spiritual discovery, not creation. The man of experience feels the presence of God and does not argue about it.

Like philosophy, religion is an attempt to account for our experience as a whole. (S. Radhakrishnan, 1967: 75) According to Radhakrishnan our concepts of nature, soul and God die, if they have no roots in experience. In the interpretation of experience, we employ method of reason. It is the only way of attaining truth. A proposition cannot be true for religion and false for reason.

Again, there is an ancient and widespread tradition that we can apprehend the Supreme Reality with directness and immediacy. Many people separated by distance of time and space have borne personal testimony to **the** experience of the Supreme Being. This direct experience is what Thomas Aquinas call ***cognitio dei experimentalis***. Everything is known to us only through experience. Even an abstract science like mathematics is based on the experience stated regularities. Philosophy of religion must therefore base itself on religious experience. The existence of God then means the real or the possible experience of this Being. If the genuine standard of knowledge is experience, we must deny that character of knowledge to our ideas of God unless they are traced by the experience of God.

Thus, according to Radhakrishnan, the assertion of the reality of God is indirect knowledge, while the experience of the reality of God is direct knowledge.

***"I am Brahman*, *Aham Brahmasmi"*** of the ***Vedic*** seers, Jesus's words concerning his divinity, ***"I am the truth," "Ana Alhaqq"*** of ***Al Hallai*** have a family resemblance. Thomas Aquinas speaks of ***"knowledge through conaturality (co-naturality)."*** Thus we have knowledge of divine reality either through theology or by personal experience. As Pseudo-Dionysins put it, we not only learn the truth but suffer it. Kierkegaard's hostility to Hegel was due to latter's conception of truth as an elaborate speculative system, claiming objective validity. For Kierkegaard, truth is to be obtained not by intellectual effort but by personal commitment. Spiritual truth is inwardness, not logical meditation. Truth is existential. To know it we must live in it. It must become a part of our being, a sort of personal depth. When Kierkegaard says that subjectivity is truth, he does not mean that man is the measure of all things. He means that truth is not truth until the seeker personally appropriates it.

Spiritual apprehension insists on a participation of the known subject in the spiritual reality, a touching (***haptus***) and testing (gustus) of the object of knowledge. We see, feel and taste the truth. This is the immediate awareness of Being itself. It is experience by participation, by a renewal of the self. We apprehend it with all sides of our being, ***Sarvabhavena***. Truth is the vision of reality which satisfies one's whole being. It is grasped by the complete man. This direct experience, Radhakrishnan says, is as old as humanity and is not limited to any one race or religion. The intimations of this type of experience are to be found not only in the realms of metaphysics religion but also in art and communion with nature.

In the personal experience of the seers of different religions, we discern characteristics which are unaffected by differences of race and geography thus illustrating an astonishing similarity in regard to spiritual life in spite of slight variations. Direct spiritual experience is a psychological state, independent of the metaphysical doctrine is not affected to the truth or falsity of the metaphysical doctrine inferred from it. Yet the experience has a cognitive value. It involves a metaphysical conception of the nature of the Absolute, the human soul and world and also a certain way of attaining union with the Absolute or God. There are varieties of expressions and variations even among those who profess the same religion. But the similarity is striking whether we take the Hindu seers, or the Buddhist teachers, or the Greek thinkers like Socrates, Plato, Aristotle and Piotinus, or the Christian mystics or the Sufis.

The interpretation is never adequate to the experience. As all knowledge presupposed the dualism between the subject and the object, we cannot regard man's essential being or the nature of Ultimate Reality as a possible object of cognitive. We cannot think of Being as object. To think of ***Being*** as object is to do violence to reality and create a fissure between the subject and the object. Being cannot be defined or shown but can only be alluded to, or indicated. The primordial Being, the primary datum, can be elucidated and not described.

To indicate that the Ultimate Reality is not an object of knowledge, many of the seers refuse to characterize the nature of it. They declare the Supreme Reality to be a mystery, a hidden secret. The more it is experienced as the inexpressible, the more it is felt to be indubitable. This knowledge, as Radhakrishnan says, does not spring from belief or a process of reasoning. It goes beyond both of them without contradicting them. Many of the seers content themselves with silent adoration, and refuse to indulge in words. They describe Him without the sound of words. ***Bahva*** tells his pupil ***Vaskali*** that the self is silence, ***Santovam Atma***. St. Augustine says that God is not even to be called ineffable because to say this is to make an assertion about Him. It is a pure silence; a soundless void (S. Radhakrishnan, 1967: 34) St. Gregory also denies the possibility of defining God as He is beyond description and thought. (S. Radhakrishnan, 1967: 136) St. Thomas also held that the final knowledge of God is tantamount to the negation of our empirical conception of Him. Thus Radhakrishnan drives home the transcendence and ineffability of religious experience.

### 4.1 Character of Religious Experience

It is a condition of consciousness in which feelings are fused, ideas tend to melt into one another, boundaries are broken and ordinary distinctions are transcended. (S. Radhakrishnan, 1971: 72) To study the nature of such experience is a difficult task according to Radhakrishnan, and all that one can hope to do is to set down a few general impressions, past and present fade away in a sense of timeless being. Consciousness and being are not there different from each other. All being is consciousness and all consciousness is being. Thought and reality are coalesced, and a creative merging of subject and object results. Life grows conscious of its incredible depths. In this fullness of spiritual freedom, the distinction of the knower and the known disappears. The privacy of the individual self is broken, and invaded by a universal self whom the individual feels as his real self.

The experience itself is felt to be sufficient and complete. It does not come in a fragmentary or truncated form, demanding completion by something else. It does not look beyond itself for meaning or validity. It does not appear to external standards of logic or metaphysics. It is its own cause and explanation. It is sovereign in its own right and carries with it, its own credentials. It is self-established ***Swatah-Siddha,*** self-evidencing ***Svasamvedva***, and self-illumining ***Svayam-Pradasa***. It does not agree or explain but it knows and does. It is beyond the bounds of proof and so touches completeness. It cores with a constraint that brooks no denial. It is pure comprehension, entire significance, and completes validity. ***Patanjali,*** the author of the ***Yoga Sutras***, tells us that the insight is truth-filled, or truth-bearing.

The tension of normal life disappears, giving rise to inward peace, power and joy. The Greek called it ***Ataravy***. The Hindu term ***'Shanti'*** or peace is similarly a positive feeling of calm and confidence, joy and strength in the midst of outward pain and defeat, loss and frustration.

The experience is felt as profoundly satisfying, turning darkness into light, sadness into joy, and despair into assurance. Since the intuitive experiences are not always given but occur only at rare intervals, they possess the character of revelation. We cannot command or continue them at our will. We do not know how or why do they occur? They sometime occur even against our will. The mode of their comprehension is traced to the supernatural. Those who are gifted with the insight, tend to regard themselves as the chosen ones, they feel inclined to believe that the light has been directed on them, and that they are not only the seekers but are also sought, ***"Only he who is chosen by the Supreme, is able to realize it."*** (S. Radhakrishnan, 1971: 74)

Even the noblest human minds, Radhakrishnan explains, have only glimpse of self-valid experience. The moments of the vision are transitory and intermittent. We, therefore, do not attain an insight, permanent and uninterrupted, where reality is present in its own immediate witness. But we are convinced that such an ideal is not an impossible one.

### 4.2 Religious Experience and the Variety of Expression.

When we test the claim of the experience to truth, we are really discussing the claims of the forms or propositions in which the nature of the experience is unfolded. (S. Radhakrishnan, 1971: 77) In the utterances of the seers, we have to distinguish between the given and the elements of interpretation. What is regarded as immediately given may be the product of the inference. Immediacy does not mean absence of psychological meditation, but only non-meditation by conscious thought. Ideas which seem to come to us with compelling force, without any mediate intellectual process, of which we are aware, are generally the results of previous training in traditions, imparted to us in our early years. Our past experience supplies the materials to which the new insight adds fresh meanings. Thus when we are told that the souls have felt in their lives the redeeming power of Krishna or Buddha, Jesus or Mohammad, we must distinguish the immediate experience or intuition which might conceivably be infallible and the interpretation which is mixed up with it. St. Theresa tells us that after undergoing mysterious experience she learned to understand the meaning of Trinity. Surely she would not have recognized the relation as that of the Trinity if she had not already known something of the Trinity. Similarly, if Paul has not learned something about Jesus, he would not have identified the voice that came to him on the Damascus road as that of Jesus.

Radhakrishnan says, we must distinguish the simple facts of religion from the accounts which reach us through theological conceptions and doctrines. That the soul is in contact with mighty spiritual power other than its normal self and yet within it and that its contact with the power means the beginning of the creation of a new life for the self is the fact, while the identification of this power with the historic figures of Buddha or Christ, or the identification of the simple realization of the universal self within us with a sudden revelation from without, is an interpretation, a personal confession, and necessarily an objective truth. Something is directly experienced, but it is unconsciously interpreted in terms of the tradition in which the individual is trained.

Again, there is no such thing as pure and uninterrupted experience. It is always mixed up with different layers of interpretation. The scriptural statements give us knowledge, or interpreted experience, that-what. The ***"that"*** is merely the affirmation of a fact, of a self-existent spiritual experience in which all distinctions are blurred and the individual seems to overflow into the whole and belong to it. The experience is real though inarticulate.

Among the religious teachers of the world, Buddha is marked out as the one who admitted the reality of the spiritual experience and yet refused to interpret it as revelation of anything beyond itself. For Buddha, according to Radhakrishnan, the experience that gives us direct contact with God is an interpretation and not an immediate datum. Buddha gives us a report of the experience rather than an interpretation of it, though strictly speaking there are no experiences which we do not interpret. Interpretation is only a question of degree. But Buddha remains faithful to the given and is content with affirming that a deeper world of spirit, penetrates the visible and the tangible world. Such a world certified as valid by the witness of perfect intuition exists **beyond** or rather within the world of multiplicity and change which the senses and understanding present to us. The primary reality is an unconditional existence beyond all potentiality of adequate expression by thought or description by **symbol**, in which the word ***"existence"*** itself loses its meaning, and the symbol of the ***Nirvana*** alone seems to be justified. The only liberty in which Buddha indulges when obliged to give a positive content to it is to identify it with Eternal righteousness (***dharma***), which is the principle of the Universe and the foundation of all conduct. It is on account of it that we have the implicit belief in the worth of life.

The ***Hindu*** thinkers admit the ineffability of the experience but permit themselves a graduated scale of interpretations from the most 'impersonal' to the most 'personal'. Hinduism admits that the unquestionable content of the experience is 'that' about which nothing more can be said. The deeper and more intimate a spiritual experience, the more readily does it dispense with signs and symbols. Deep intuition is utterly silent. Through silence we ***"confess without confession"*** that the glory of spiritual life is inexplicable and beyond the reach of speech and mind. It is the great unfathomable mystery and words are treacherous.

### 4.3 God and Self

Radhakrishnan asserts that there is in the self of man, or at the very center of his being, something deeper than the intellect, which is skin to the Supreme. (S. Radhakrishnan, 1971: 81) God's revelation and man's contemplation are two sides of the same fact. In the spiritual experience itself, the barrier between the self and the ultimate reality drops away. In the moment of its highest insight, the self becomes aware not only of its own existence but of the existence of an omnipresent spirit of which it is, as it were, a focus, we belong to the real, and the real is mirrored in us. Radhakrishnan refers to the Upanishadic saying ***Tat Tvamasi*** (***That is Thou***) as attesting to the above fact. He compares this with Plato's theory of self which maintains the latter's participation in an eternal mode of being He also notes the similarity of the Upanishadic doctrines of self with those of Plotinus and Descartes. He quotes William James to the effect that the overcoming of the barrier between the individual and Absolute is central to all mystic traditions (S. Radhakrishnan, 1971 : 82 -83) Regarding the two fold aspects of Divinity,

Radhakrishnan explains that the difference between the Supreme as spirit and the Supreme as Person is one of the standpoint and not of essence. The difference is between God as He is and God as He seems to us. When we consider the abstract and impersonal aspects of the Supreme, we call it the Absolute; when we consider the Supreme as self-aware and self-blissful being, we get God. The real is beyond all conceptions of personality and impersonality. We call it the ***'Absolute'*** to show the sense of inadequacy of all our terms and definitions. We call it ***'God'*** to show that it is the basis of all that exists, and the goal of all personalities is a symbol and if we ignore its symbolic character, it is likely to shut us from the truth. Even those who regard personality as the ultimate category of the Universe recognize that God is vast and mysterious, mighty and ultimate. Aristotle's view of the Unmoved First Hover whose supreme perfection draws the Universe towards himself as the beauty of beloved draws the lover, and Spinoza's conception of God who is the Power before which nothing is more real, which we are called upon to love without expecting anything in return, point in the same direction. A Personal God is a creature of the religious needs of the human heart and an ethical God is the highest good at which men aim. The monotheists are quite certain that the gods of polytheists are symbolic if not mythological presentations of the true God, but they both admit that their conception of God is at the bottom of symbol. All religions are symbolic, and symbolism is excluded from religion only when religion itself perishes. (S. Radhakrishnan, 1971: 84-85) God is a symbol in and through which religion sees the Absolute. Philosophers may quarrel about the Absolute and God, and content that God, the Holy One Who is worshipped, is different from the Absolute, which is the reality demonstrated by reason. But to the religious consciousness the two are one.

The seers of all religions, Radhakrishnan points out, agree that there is something in the human soul, which is related to the Absolute, or is the Absolute. It is the original ground of the soul, the meeting point of soul and God, the source and basis of all knowledge, all beauty, all goodness, indeed of all ideas of universal significance. The soul can know the Transcendent Reality when it descends into its deepest centre because it is one with the Reality. It is there identical with what it knows. According to Radhakrishnan, when the Upanishads proclaim the great truth, ***"That are Thou"***, when the Buddha teaches, ***"Each human individual has in him the power to grow into a Buddha or a Bodhisattva"***, when Jesus tell his hearers, ***"The Kingdom of Heavens is within them"*** and when Mohammad affirms, ***"God is hearer to us than the very artery of our neck",*** they all mean that the most important thing in life is not to be found in anything external to man but is to be found in the bidden strata of this thought and being. We must not look for it outside of us. (S. Radhakrishnan, 1967: 136-137)

## 4.4 Religion and Symbolism

Radhakrishnan asserts that the Real has been conceived in many ways through religious symbolism. We express our felt-experience in propositions that are symbolical. We communicate the experience to those who have not had it through what is already known to them. A true symbol is not a dream or a shadow. It is the living revelation of the Unfathomable. The ***Vedic*** seems and the followers of Zarathustra look upon fire (***Agni***)) as the symbol of the Supreme. The brightness of the effulgent Reality suggests to us the image of the burning fire. The ***Upanishads*** call it the light or lights, ***Inotisam Ivotih***. Boohme and William Law speak of it as the Divine Light. Radhakrishnan tells us that the different symbolical representations bring out varied aspects of the Supreme (S. Radhakrishnan. 1967 : 140-141) Thomas Aquinas adopted from Aristotle the principle of ***"analogy"*** or a measure of likeness between man and God, between human reason and Divine Truth. We accept the dogma or the symbol through faith, which is for most people the **only** possible mode of participation in the divine truth.

The forms and symbols are ways to help us to an inward realization. All the time, the seers are aware that human language breaks down **when** it attempts to expound the nature of Ultimate Reality. The variety of symbolism for Radhakrishnan is due not to the nature of the experience as such, but to the prevailing theological or **metaphysical** conceptions. These colour the expectation of the seer and form the background through which he interprets his illumination. The symbols and dogmas are not definitive. Eastern forms of religion hold that differences of interpretation do not affect the one universal truth any more than the differences of colour effect the uncoloured light. Western forms of religion are inclined to hold that one definition or one interpretation of reality is final and absolute, and others are false.

In India, Radhakrishnan says, each definition represents a ***Darshana*** or a viewpoint. There are many ways of viewing one experience. The different ***Darshana*** are different viewpoints which are not necessarily incompatible. They are pointers on the way to spiritual realization. If religious truth is seen by different groups in different ways, it is not to deny that truth is ultimately one. If there are resemblances in higher religions, they are to be welcomed as the expressions of the working of the mysterious spirit of God at sundry times in diverse manners, binding them all together in a single bond.

According to Radhakrishnan, to attain spiritual insight inward piety, certain forms and rites are prescribed. The body of doctrine, myth, rite, cult and worship form the objective side of religion. These may differ in different religions but behind all these there is the tendency to attain spiritual realization. We have to accept these forms to communicate the universal truths to those who are in a particular stage of history. Thus what is permanent and universal is translated into something temporary and local. Tradition and environment condition are both the vision of Reality and its presentation. These expressions cannot be stationary. Truth is not something given once and for all. Truth may be divine in its inspiration but it is always expressed in human form. Professor A.H. Whitehead says; ***"The trouble with the Bible has been its interpreters, who have sealed and whittled down that sense of infinite into finite and limited concepts and the first interpreter of the New Testament was the worst, Paul."*** (S. Radhakrishnan. 1970: 54-55)

All religions are to be viewed as varied manifestation of the true religion. Even those who acknowledge the existence of God admit the inadequacy of human ideas to express Him. What the atheist denies is an idea of God, but not God Himself. What an theist affirms is not an idea of God, but God Himself. We should not, therefore, transfer the Absoluteness which belongs to Divine Reality to its historical formulations.

## 4.5 Religion and Science

Radhakrishnan acknowledges the fact that

religion as it is generally understood, is opposed to the spirit of science (K. M. Munshi and R. R. Diwakar, 1969 : 87) The method of science is empirical while that of religion is dogmatic. Science does not rely on authority but appeals to communicable evidence that any trained mind can evaluate. Science does not admit to any barriers to freedom of thought and inquiry. It welcomes new knowledge and new experience. A true scientist does not take refuge in dogmatism. His outlook is marked by modesty, self-criticism and readiness to learn from others. If we esteem freedom of inquiry, we find that it is incompatible with authoritarianism, which is the dominant feature of religion. For science, all judgments are provisional and subject to revision in light or fresh knowledge. If established religions become rigid, closed and confined narrowly to the world whose boundaries are marked out in the scriptures written centuries ago, those attracted by the scientific method, which has demonstrated its validity, not only theoretically but practically, through the spectacular technological results, are inclined to prefer the laboratory to the altar.

Actually a true understanding of science, according to Radhakrishnan, supports a religion of spirit. Science is not an entirely self-moving process; or an unconscious instrument of historical change. The development of science is due to the genuineness of the individual who has knowledge, skills and values. Man is not master of the Universe because he can split the atom because he has that in him which is far superior to the atom. The conflict between science and religion, as Radhakrishnan sees it, is due to historical circumstances. In the past, scientists have suffered from religious and political tyrannies. Giordano Bruno was burnt at the stake, Galileo was imprisoned and threatened and even today scientists are discouraged by threats of political inquisition or moral ostracism from speaking the truth. Scientists must stand against all tyranny, determined to preserve the integrity of science and prevent its perversion from its proper beneficent use and save civilization from misusing science for its own destruction. God is truth, and the service of truth is the service of God.

Both religion and science affirm the unity of nature. The central assumption of science closes to the intuition of religion namely that nature is intelligible. When we study the processes of nature we are impressed by their order and harmony and are led to a belief in the divine reality. As St. Thomas said that by considering what God has made we can-first of all catch a glimpse of divine wisdom which has in some measure impressed a certain likeness to itself upon them. (K. M. Munshi and R. R. Diwakar, 1969: 424)

Science is empirical, it is non-dogmatic. If scientific truth is confirmed in experience, religious truth also can be put to the same test. If we take the raw material of human nature and process it through detachment, humility and love, knowledge of God is attained. As Albert Schweitzer observes it is rational thinking which is free from assumptions and ends in mysticism (K. M. Munshi and R. R. Diwakar, 1969: 426).

Religious people of all denomination are increasingly accepting the Eastern emphasis on religion as experience of life. It is not faith but works that are needed.

Comparing religious knowledge with scientific knowledge, Radhakrishnan says that while scientific knowledge is the result of logical deduction and analysis of accumulated data, religious knowledge is one by revelation. (S. Radhakrishnan, 1967: 74) Moses was long troubled by the problem of saving the children of Israel and suddenly had a revelation by the burning bush. Gautama, the Buddha enquired for years about the nature of reality, and one day while being in meditation quietly under The Bodhi' tree, he realized the truth. Archimedes leapt from his bath with a triumphant ***"Eureka"***, having seen in a sudden flash the scientific principle which had long eluded him in his study. After hard work and intellectual commitment to a problem, the scientist suddenly sees the answer by a revelation, as it were.

In both religion and science, it is more an imaginative leap than the mere accumulation of facts that lead to discovery and creation. In science the test is fidelity to the observed data which is the measure of the validity of theories. The habit of truth runs deep in the scientist's mind, and it will be always willing to reject established dogma when experience suggests a new truth. Both science and religion promote the sense of human dignity.

Radhakrishnan thinks that the nature of proof is not different in science and religion. Where we cannot prove, we believe. Without the adoption of a working hypothesis, our mind is helpless and dumb. We devise experiments to test the validity of working hypothesis. Religious ideas are also tested and judged by the lives and experiences of those who adopt them. There is an essential similarity of purpose both in science and religion in seeking truth. The conflict between them is due largely to misunderstanding of the methods of science and failure to appreciate the deepest insight of religion.

Moreover, Radhakrishnan thinks that positive ideas help us to redeem religion from magic, superstition, and folklore with which it got confused.

While it liberates us from religious obscurantism, it should not become a form of scientific obscurantism which distorts science itself by imposing on it wrong ideas of exactitude and verification.

Radhakrishnan believes that it is no use

repudiating the religious implications of science. (S. Radhakrishnan, 1928: 8) The growing dissatisfaction with established religion, for him, is the prelude to the rise of a truer, more spiritual and so more universal religion. The scientific temper is also opposed to the acceptance of dogma. The scientist pursues truth without any bias. He does not start with the idea that his conclusions should square with certain dogmas.

Religion as dogma has no appeal to the believer in science. If religion starts with the assumption of an absolute God and tries to infer his characteristics, the nature of the world, etc., from its initial assumption, it tends to become mere scholasticism or deductive development of dogma. If there is an omnipotent and beneficent God, then the world which is his creation must be good. Evil is only an appearance. The suffering of the wicked is God's judgment and the suffering of the righteous is God's test. Science has no sympathy with such a ***priori*** schemes of revealed religion. It starts not so much with the creator as with the creation. It studies the facts of nature and society and frames an idea of God to suit them. It approaches the problems of religion with an attitude of empiricism or experimentalism. Therefore, rightly understood, Radhakrishnan says, science is essentially spiritual in its temper and leanings. Instead of abolishing the mysteries of the world, it has deepened them.

Among the new forces that have made our

world so different from what it was, the most important is natural science (S. Radhakrishnan, 1971: 12) The strict method of science requires us to believe a proposition only when we are in a position to prove it whenever statements are made, it is our duty to find out whether they are capable of verification by those who will make the trouble to investigate them.

If for science truth is something, we are getting nearer and nearer as time goes on, for religion it need not be different. We need not think that in religion truth is something, handed down from the past. The golden age is in the future vision, not in a fabled past. Our scientific theories which supersede earlier ones are only links on a long chain of progressive advance likely in time to be themselves transcended. Their only justification is their adequacy. They are temporary resting places in the search for truth and there is nothing absolute about them. Religion also should not claim to be absolutistic.

Science insists on the reign of law. If law works everywhere and through all time, there is nothing mysterious or miraculous about the world. The world is cosmos, and ordered whole. While in the West this conception was suggested by the astronomical discoveries of the fourth century B. C. in India, the law of the Universe the ***Rita*** was accepted as early as the ***Vedic*** Period.

Religious thinkers offer proofs for the existence

of God. We find them in the Upanishads, in Plato and in Aristotle. (S. Radhakrishnan, 1967: 73) St. Thomas Aquinas" five proofs are well known. Kant bases his theistic conviction on the nature of human conscience and Hegel on the nature of the rational thought. Religion should satisfy our instinct for truth. God is truth. He is ***Satvasvarupa***. He is of the nature of truth, and as Gandhi puts it. 'Truth' is God. This statement is a commentary on the ***Upanishadic*** text, ***Tapo Brahma***. Sincere and reverent thinking is itself divine. The Buddha insists that reason based on evidence is our only guide to truth. He asks us not to believe in any sacred book because of its antiquity. Each one should search for truth himself, think for himself, and realise the truth for himself. Jesus affirms that the spirit of truth is in us and when realized it will make us free (S. Radhakrishnan, 19 : 73) When Jesus asks us to love God with our whole being, He means that we should love Him with our intellect also. What is required of us is intelligent, but not sentimental love.

In all circumstances, truth is more valuable than its opposition, whether we are scientists or religious men; we are committed unreservedly to the search for truth. Science is not sentiment, nor is religion dogma. The truth which science offers us will make us see greater depth in religion.

Science becomes superstition, if it frees its votaries from the duty of independent thought. About the middle of the nineteenth century, science became as dogmatic as any religion. It assumed that the world and everything within it is an elaborate mechanism in which everything is resolvable finally into hard material particles. Such a mechanistic interpretation excluded any genuine possibility for the rise and development of the values of mind and spirit.

Modern science, as Radhakrishnan interprets is not committed to the mechanistic materialist view. (S. Radhakrishnan, 1968: 156) Scientific statements are valid only within the framework of strictly limited relations. While they study the working of atoms and electrons, they do not and cannot say anything about the creation of atoms and electrons. The scientist who is a part of the Universe cannot as a scientist make any statement about the meaning of the Universe as a whole.

Philosophical theories arise out of reflection on the given data. The ***Brahma Sutras*** open with the words, ***Athato Brahma Jijnasa***. (S. Radhakrishnan, 1968: 187) Now, therefore, an enquiry into Brahma the next sutra tells us that the Supreme Spirit is the basis of the world process, its origin, maintenance and dissolution. The underlying structure of reality is accessible to reason because it is the product of reason. Nature is not self-subsistent but owes its being to a transcendent principle whose mind is reflected, though freely, in it. This world is God's world:

***Isavasyam Idam Sarvam***. (S. Radhakrishnan, 1968: 187) This makes discoveries of an ultimate principle which underlines and informs the cosmic process is not only inferred but is also intuited. Experience is not limited to the facts of space and time. We have experience of law of nature, of universal also of Ultimate Reality.

Radhakrishnan reminds us that the soul's direct contact in full awareness of Transcendent Reality is a basic postulate of both Eastern and Western thought. Plato sees in the soul a being of divine origin; In it is the longing for reunion with the Divine. St. Paul's Damascus experience is an illustration of spiritual certainty. Augustine's words are well known when he said my mind is the flash of trembling glance came to Absolute that which is. (S. Radhakrishnan, 1968: 158)

Many seers have testified to the vision of beauty and the meaning in the heart of things. H. G. Wells in First and Last Things wrote At times in the silence of the night and in rare, lonely moments I come upon a sort of communion of myself and something which is not I. These moments happen and they are supreme facts in my religious life. They are the crown of my religious experience. (S. Radhakrishnan, 968: 158)

Radhakrishnan believes that under the influence of the universal experiences of religion and modem science and technology, mankind is being moulded into a single community. Science will triumph over ignorance and superstition and religion over selfishness and fear and nations will come together to build a great future for humanity, the brotherhood of man which has been the vision of the prophets since the beginning of time.

A scientific study of religion from Radhakrishnan's point of view, takes issue with the idea that religion is real only in religions which are particular and concrete. (S. Radhakrishnan, 1970: 50) The empirical fact of the plurality of religions, each with its own peculiar character and structure, should not hide from us the transcendent unity of religions. The vital differences among the living faiths of mankind are over-arched by a fundamental unity of vision and purpose which embraces all mankind.

According to Radhakrishnan, all religions affirm that man is confronted by something greater than himself, which, in contrast to human nature and all other phenomena, is Absolute Reality. It is the transcendent, the Divine, the true being behind, the ground and substance of all existence.

The Absolute Reality is also the Absolute Good for which man is a thirst. This transcendent Reality is immanent in the human soul. The human spirit is grounded in Godhead. The ***Upanishadic*** saying 'That thou art,' refers to this fact of Divine Immanence. The essence of Buddha is present in every being. 'Kingdom of God is within you,' According to Jesus, For St. Augustine, God is 'more inward than my innermost being'. The Quran says that God is nearer to us than our artery in the neck. Religion and science, faith and reason represent different sides of human nature. Each one of us is both religious and scientific.

### 4.6 Faith and Religion

Radhakrishnan quotes with approval Wesley's following saying that Faith is the vision of the soul, that power by which spiritual things are apprehended, just as material things are apprehended by the physical senses He continues: ***"We call it faith simply because spiritual perception, like other kinds of perceptions, is liable to error and requires the testing processes of logical thought."*** (Paul Arthur Schilpp, 1952: 220)

According to Radhakrishnan, faith (***Shraddha***) is the basis of ***Bhakti***. So the gods in whom people have faith are tolerated. Some love, says Radhakrishnan, is better than none, for if we do not love we become shut up within ourselves. Besides, the lower gods are accepted as forms of the One Supreme. However there is insistence on the fact that **only** he who is devoted to the Supreme, reaches to the infinite bliss. (S. Radhakrishnan, 1976: 64) So long as worship is done with devotion, it purifies the heart and prepares the mind for the higher consciousness.

The ***Chandogva Upanishad*** says ***'Shraddha***

***Tapah***.' Faith is asceticism. Accordingly, Radhakrishnan says that to realize freedom from the bondage of outward things, one need not go to the forest to increase his privations and penances. (S. Radhakrishnan, 1948:216)

For Radhakrishnan, religion rests on faith. (S. Radhakrishnan, 1974: 14) He does not. However, agree with the mechanical conception of faith which depends on authority without any experience of being religious. This kind of faith, says Radhakrishnan, is quite different from the religious faith which has its roots in experience. He quotes Wesley who asks, ***"What is faith?"*** and answers, ***"neither an opinion nor any number of opinions put together, be they so very true. It is the vision of the soul, that power by which spiritual things are apprehended, just as material things are apprehended by the physical senses."*** (S. Radhakrishnan, 1974:14)

Blind belief in dogmas is not the faith which saves. It is an unfortunate legacy of the curse which Christian theology has followed in Europe that faith has come to connote a mechanical adherence to authority. According to Radhakrishnan, if we take faith in the proper sense of spiritual conviction, then religion is based on faith or intuition. We call it faith simply because spiritual perception, like other kinds of perception, is liable to error and requires the testing processes of logical thought. But, like all perception, religious intuition is that which though has to start from and to which it has to return. In order to be able to say that religious experience reveals Reality, and in order to be able to transform religious certitude into logical certainty, we are obliged to give an intellectual account of the experience.

As .interpreted by Radhakrishnan, the ***Vedic Mantras*** are addressed to various powers, symbolic of important aspects, of the Supreme Reality. (S. Radhakrishnan, 1953: 131) They teach the religion of ***Shradha*** (faith) and Upasana (worship). Both these methods are taken up by the ***Upanishads*** and are reinterpreted. The different forms of ***Shraddha*** or faith, ***Upasana*** or worship, and practices of yoga are treated as means to the supreme and of self-knowledge (***atma-darsana***) which is at once a union with the one transcendent Being beyond all the worlds, and a union with all beings in the world.

Radhakrishnan points out that ***Shraddha*** or faith plays an important role and is quite necessary for religious life because it is the first step to learn what has been thought and said about religious experience from teachers. We should listen to them with ***Shraddha*** or faith. (S. Radhakrishnan, 1953: 133) For him, faith is an act of will. It is the heart that matters rather not the intellectual disposition. It is astikya-Buddhi as Shankara calls it. We should have faith in the integrity of the seers whose selflessness has enabled them to know the nature of Ultimate Reality by direct acquaintance. The propositions they have formulated from out of their personal experience, give us knowledge by description, as we do not yet have direct vision of the truth, yet the knowledge we so acquire is not unverifiable. The truth of the Vedic propositions can be verified by us, if we are prepared to fulfill the necessary conditions. Hence, ***Shraddha*** as defined by Radhakrishnan is an essential stage, preparatory to God-vision (***Brahma-Saksatkara***) always with other stages like ***Shravana*** (hearing), ***Manana*** (reflection) and ***Nididdhyasana*** (contemplation).

In the stage of ***Manana*** or reflection we attempt to form clear ideas by logical processes of inference, analogy, etc. So long as faith is firm, says Radhakrishnan, the need for philosophy increases. Unquestioning belief in the inherent power of knowledge underlines the intellectual fabric of the ***Upanishads***. Radhakrishnan further states that the truth of the Vedantic propositions can also be inferred by us by reasoning process. Hearing of the scriptures is not devoid of intellectual content. One who hears he understands up to a point. But when he reflects on what he hears, he adds to faith a knowledge which increases faith. There is great insistence on the need for logical inquiry. Without it faith will degenerate into credulity. However, without the material supplied by faith, logical reasoning may turn into mere speculation. While the scriptures declared the truth by enunciation, philosophy establishes it by argument.

The third stage of ***Nididdhyasana*** is the process by which intellectual consciousness is transformed into a vital one. We concentrate on the truth here. Faith then becomes real in us by the steady concentration of mind on Reality (S. Radhakrishnan, 1953: 135).

Accordingly Radhakrishnan says that the field of faith is that which surpasses reason. Faith gives due recognition to mystery. (S. Radhakrishnan, 1960: 108 -110) He very aptly sums up his position in this context that there is an Indian saying that words are the daughters of earth but deeds are the sons of heaven. Words are born of intellect, deeds of spirit. It is faith that can move mountains. Faith is an attitude of will, the energy of soul, the response of the entire self, in faith we believe not only with our brains but with our whole soul and body. The idea is not merely thought out but grows from the deepest layers of life and mind. (S. Radhakrishnan, 1967: 93)

According to Radhakrishnan, though faith and belief are different, they are not in conflict. An act of faith involves surrendering to the creative intuition which transcends the limited awareness of the intellectual self. (S. Radhakrishnan, 1960 : 116) He observes that those who live by faith, who had a personal encounter with the Supreme, need not abandon the traditional formulations of belief in which they have been reared, for these beliefs were also originally born in the mind of man. However, to become organic expressions of faith they must be reborn and continually renewed in personal experience. Even when we admit revelation, there must be an answering witness within the soul. The highest reality has to be assumed or taken on faith till it reveals itself in the devotee's consciousness. (S. Radhakrishnan, 1948: 562) The problem of meaningfulness or meaninglessness of religious beliefs cannot be solved by faith alone (S. Radhakrishnan, 1970: 32) The faith has to be sustained by metaphysical knowledge. We have to think out the metaphysical presuppositions and attain personal experience of the religious a ***priori*** from which all living faiths start. We need intellectual effort and spiritual apprehension, that is to say both metaphysics and religion. Only reasoned faith can give coherence to life and thought. The insights of the Scriptures require to be clarified by the use of reason. The worlds of reason and of religion do not move in different orbits. Indian thought, according to Radhakrishnan, is firm in its conviction that religious propositions should be strengthened and confirmed by reason.

## 4.7 Intuition and Religion

Radhakrishnan uses the term 'intuition' to tell that faculty which lies within the self, as an endowment of its fundamental nature; it is also subject to cultivation. Intuition in many of Radhakrishnan's usages seems to involve quality as when he says mat in intuition ***"we see things as they are, as unique individuals."*** In it there is a ***"close communion between the knower and the known."*** (Paul Arthur Schilpp, 1952: 178 -179)

Radhakrishnan sometimes uses the term in a way which seems to deny quality viz intuitive knowledge arises from an intimate fusion of mind with reality. It is knowledge by being and not by senses or by symbols. It is awareness of the truth of things by identity. We become one with the truth, one with the object of knowledge. Radhakrishnan uses the word ***"intuition"*** in different senses, Professor Robert W. Browing gives an excellent analysis of Radhakrishnan's usage, which is some times it intimates what cannot be known in other ways: sometimes it means a fuller 'realization' of what may be already abstractly known in symbols; sometimes it is attached to the dawning, in the mind of the discoverer, of what will be, after confirmation, a powerful scientific generalization; sometimes it denotes the knowledge of individual things in their concreteness; sometimes it is referring to Intuitive knowledge of the One Real. Sometimes it is accepting the dynamism of thinking as against the result; sometimes it is emphasizing a spontaneous dynamism as against movement which may be automatic or mechanical. (Paul Arthur Schilpp, 1952: 177 -178)

Radhakrishnan speaks of intuitive knowing. This kind of knowing, as he describes, it is quite different from conceptual knowing. It is non-sensuous, immediate knowledge. According to him, intuitive knowledge arises from an intimate fusion of mind with reality. It is knowledge by being, and not gained by means of senses or by symbols. It is awareness of the truth of things by identity. We become one with the truth, one with the object of knowledge. The object known here is seen not as- an object outside the self, but as a part of the self. What intuition reveals is not so much a doctrine as a consciousness; it is a state of mind and not a definition of the object. (S. Radhakrishnan, 1971: 108-110)

The great illustration of intuitive knowledge given by Hindu thinkers is the knowledge of self. We become aware of our own selves, as we become aware of love or anger, directly by a sort of identity. Therefore, self-knowledge is inseparable from self-existence. It seems to be the only true and direct knowledge we have; all else is inferential. For ***Shankara*** as Radhakrishnan sees it, self-knowledge which is neither logical nor sensuous is the presupposition of every other kind of knowledge. It alone is beyond doubt for ***"it is of the essential nature of him who denies it."*** (S. Radhakrishnan, 1971: 109)

Intuitive self-knowledge knows itself as a single indivisible act of knowledge, an act which is one with its self-existence. It is through intuitive understanding or sympathetic interpretation that we know other minds. (S. Radhakrishnan, 1971: 112) The deepest things of life are known only through intuitive apprehension. We recognize their truth but do not reason about them. In the sphere of values also we depend a good deal on this kind of knowledge. Both the recognition and creation of values are due to intuitive understanding.

Intuitive truths, according to Radhakrishnan, as simple acts of mental vision are free from doubt. They do not carry conviction on the ground of their logical validity. We cannot help assenting to them as soon as we intuit them. If intuitive knowledge is knowledge by coincidence or identity, the possession of the intuitive knowledge of reality means that it is possible for us to coincide or be one with reality. If our nature is spirit, so is the real. Though intuition lies beyond intellect, it is not contrary to it. It is called ***Samvagjnana*** or perfect knowledge. Reflective understanding is a preparation for this integral experience. ***Shankara,*** says Radhakrishnan, observes that the fruit of knowledge is manifest to intuition. Radhakrishnan explains that intuition is not logical but supra-logical. It is the wisdom gained by the whole spirit which is above any mere fragment thereof, be it feeling or intellect. The whole life of mind is more concrete than that of any specialized mode of it. It follows that the great intuitions bear the stamp of personality. According to him, intuitive knowledge is not non-rational; it is only non-conceptual. (S.

Radhakrishnan, 1971: 120) In it both immediacy and mediacy comprehend. As a matter of fact, we have, throughout our lives, the intuitive and the intellectual aspects in us working together. Even in pure mathematics where the conclusion is not evident, until the datas are brought together and set forth on logical sequence, there is an element of intuition.

Anyway, all intuitions are involved in self-knowledge, according to Radhakrishnan. 119 All growth in knowledge is an elaboration of intuition, an increasing assimilation of the mind of man to the spirit in him. All experience issues forth from it and rests in it. It is beyond the reach of mind and the sense, though the mind and the senses are illumined or inspired by it, as he quotes from the ***Upanishad***. (S. Radhakrishnan, 1971:123)

Thus Radhakrishnan accords prominence to religious experience in the phenomenon of religion. He does not underestimate the utility of reason but rejects all claims of finality about it. He has vehemently contended for the place of mystery faith and intuition in the religious life of man. Being a modern Hindu thinker he delves deeper into the common religious foundation of human culture and explores the basic features of a world faith.

❖❖❖

## Chapter III

# RADHAKRISHNAN'S UNDERSTANDING OF HINDUISM

### 1. Meaning and scope of Hinduism

In the long and continuous Hindu tradition ***Truth*** is realized through real knowledge from the time of the Upanishads down to Tagore and Gandhi. However, there can be various kinds of expression of Truth. Hinduism, according to Radhakrishnan, fully realizes that fact. For Hinduism has always stood for developing an attitude of comprehensive charity, instead of insisting on a fanatic faith in an inflexible creed. It accepted a multiplicity of aboriginal gods and goddesses that originates, most of them, outside the ***Aryan*** tradition, and justified them all. Again, it is characteristic of Hinduism to respect and have good will for other creeds. (S. Radhakrishnan, 1974: 28)

For Radhakrishnan, Hinduism may be regarded as the first example of a missionary religion. Worshippers of different gods and followers of different rites were taken into the Hindu fold. As the ancient practice of ***Vratvatoms*** describes fully in the ***Tandya Brahmana*** shows not only individuals but whole tribes were absorbed to

***Hinduism***. The ***Hindu*** method of religious reform as Radhakrishnan sees is essentially democratic. It allows each group to get to the truth through its own tradition by means of discipline of mind and morals. Hence, he says, to despise people's gods is to despise the people, for they and their gods are adapted to each other[1]. Therefore, the Hindu took up the gods of even the savages and the uncivilized, and set them on equal thrones to his own.

Radhakrishnan gives an analogical picture in the development of the concept of ***Yahveh*** in the Pentateuch. (S. Radhakrishnan, 1974: 32-33)

In Hinduism whenever a new cult is accepted into itself, the name is retained though a refinement of the content is effected. To take an example from the early Sanskrit literature, it is clear that ***Kali*** in her various forms is a non-Aryan goddess. But she had been gradually identified with the supreme godhead. Similarly ***Krana*** becomes the highest Godhead on the ***Bhagavad-Gita*** whatever his past origin might have been.

Thus every God accepted by ***Hinduism*** is elevated and ultimately identified with the central Reality which is one with the deeper self of man. Therefore, the addition of new gods to the ***Hindu*** pantheon does not endanger it. The identity of content signified by the different names is conveyed to the people at large by an identification of names. Accordingly the many name of ***Brahma, Vishnu,***

***Shiva Krana, Kali, Buddha*** and other historical names are used indiscriminately for Absolute Reality.

***Hinduism*** insists on the development of men's conscience and his sensibility to truth. It does not believe on bringing about a mechanical uniformity of belief and form of worship by a forcible elimination of all that is not in agreement with a particular creed. It does not believe in any statutory methods of salvation. The scheme of salvation is not limited to those who hold a particular view of God's nature and follow a particular form of worship. For Radhakrishnan such an exclusive absolution is inconsistent with the conceptual with an all-loving universal God. Hence it is not fair to God or man to assume that some people are the chosen people of God, and that their religion occupies a central place in the religious development of mankind.

***Hinduism*** seeks to achieve the unity of religions not in terms of common creed but in a common quest, This Hindu spirit is catching up in modern terms. The different religions are learning slowly to hold out heads of friendship to each other in every part of the world. The study of comparative religion is helping to develop a friendly attitude among religions toward dialogue. The parliaments of religions and conference and congresses of liberal thinkers of all creeds are trying to establish mutual understanding and harmony among different religions.

According to Radhakrishnan, ***Hinduism*** represents an effort at comprehensiveness and co-operation. It recognizes the diversity in man's approach towards, and realization of, the one Supreme Reality. For it, the essence of religion consists in man's hold on what is eternal and immanent in all. There is no fired creed by which Hinduism may be said to stand or fall, for according to it the spirit will outgrow the creed. Radhakrishnan cites the example of Sri Ramakrishna who in his spiritual life practiced different forms of belief and worship and attained spiritual perfection through them all. This shows the spiritual value of ***Hinduism*** which offers every kind of support to seekers of spiritual freedom, and brings them all to the recognition of the one transcendent truth. It is only when we dispute over theological dogmas and definition, we are divided. But when we take to the religious life of prayer and contemplation, we are brought together. The deeper, the prayer, the more is the individual lost in the apprehension of the Supreme. The hardness of the apt melts; the tentativeness of the creed is revealed, and the intense focusing of all souls is one utter Being, is grasped.

According to Radhakrishnan, Hinduism is not bound up with a creed or a book, a prophet or a founder. It is a persistent search for truth on the basis of a continuously renewed experience. It is human thought about God in continuous evolution.

There is thus no end to its prophets and seers, no limits to its communicable books. It welcomes all new experiences and new expressions of truth. Using the metaphors of light and rose, he says that light shines in whatever lamp it may burn, and a rose is beautiful in whatever garden it may bloom, hi the ***Hindu*** view of life, the worldly and the temporal are not reflected. It recognizes the ethical, the economic, the artistic and the spiritual, end of life. This shows that the social obligations are emphasized in the Hindu view of life.

Radhakrishnan quotes from the ***Isha-Upanishad,*** which says that action and knowledge of the Supreme are to be rendered and accomplished together by the seeker of perfection. (S. Radhakrishnan, 1947: 72).

With regard to image worship Radhakrishnan says that it does propose to help the development of the religious spirit within man. (S. Radhakrishnan, 1947: 123) This ultimately leads to the recognition of the Supreme who has His temple in all beings? Radhakrishnan approvingly quotes from the ***Bhagvad-Gita*** in which Lord Krishna says, ***"I am present in all beings as their soul, but ignoring my presence the mortal makes a display of image worship."*** (S. Radhakrishnan, 1947: 123)

As Radhakrishnan says, we return to image worship when we have not attained spiritual maturity to realize the presence of the Supreme everywhere and anywhere. While doing one's duty, one should worship Me the Lord in images and the like, only so long as one does not in one's heart realise Me as established in all beings. (S. Radhakrishnan, 1947: 124)

Images and their worship are for the feeble-minded, for the sages see the Supreme everywhere. The uneducated have a natural leaning to image worship, but its subordinate character should not be overlooked. Thus seeing the presence of God in all is the highest kind of religion, those who have not yet realized it, are required to practice meditation, worship, etc. For those who are unable to rise to the highest level, image worship may be useful and for them offerings and pilgrimages are advised. (S. Radhakrishnan, 1947: 124)

The spirit of worship must be embodied in religious rituals and institutions, and the religious life of a community must be given sensible and institutional expression. Without them, Radhakrishnan thinks that worship seldom develops its full richness and power. It is by means of sacred objects and ceremonial acts that man's worship gets rooted in the concrete facts of life, and develops the power to change life itself. The temple ceremonial, the different items of worship, pilgrimages, are the vehicles of unspoken convictions. Temples for him are the visible symbols of ***Hindu*** religion. They are earth's prayers to heaven. They are situated in solitary and impressive places. The practice of going to the river bank at the break of dawn, in order to worship, is being observed in ***Hinduism*** for many centuries. In his analysis, the temple rituals are meant to predispose the mind for feeling the mysterious presence of God. He disapproves animal sacrifices but approves of flowers and incense to the deities in the temples. Even in the ***Rig-Veda***, it is said that devout offerings of praise, or fuel sticks or cooked food, are as good as sacrifices. (S. Radhakrishnan, 1947: 126) The spirit of ***Hinduism***, he says, is kept alive by family worship in the home where woman plays a leading part. The ***Bhagavatas***, the trained story-tellers and recites, travel from village to village expounding the classics; the Acharyas, or the heads of ascetic orders, preserve the tradition and propagate it and also train the young. The chief support of ***Hindu*** religion has been the prophet. Unlike other religions, he comes from nowhere and is supported by no authority. As Radhakrishnan claims that India has had an unbroken succession of these prophets in every part of the country from the ***rishis*** of the ***Upanishads*** to the Buddha, Ramakrishna and Gandhi.

Radhakrishnan fully regards those characteristics of Hinduism which has always been tolerant of creeds. According to him ***Hinduism*** has the pride of place in this regard. We cannot worship the Absolute whom none agrees with the worship of personal God with form by the Hindus, for he says one has seen or can see who dwells in the light that no man can approach unto. The formless (***Nrakaram***) Absolute is conceived as formed (***Akaravat***) for the purposes of worship. Worship of God is not a deliberate alliance with falsehood, since God is the form in which alone the Absolute can be pictured by the finite mind. The highest reality appears to the individual, who has not felt its oneness with his own nature, as possessing a number of perfection. The conception of a personal God is the fusion of the highest logical truth with the deepest religious conviction. This personal God is an object of genuine worship and reverence, and not a non-ethical deity indifferent to man's needs and fears. He regarded as creator, governor and judge of the universe, possessing the qualities of power and justice, righteousness and mercy, omnipresence, omnipotence and omniscience (S. Radhakrishnan, 1948: 649)

Radhakrishnan traces the history of Hindu religious tolerance from the Harappa and Mohanjodaro civilization to the present day. ***"Toleration"***, he says, ***"is the homage which the finite mind pays to the inexhaustibility of the infinite."*** (S .Radhakrishnan, 1975: 317) The ***Vedic*** and ***Upanishadic*** religion, Buddhism as represented by Ashoka, the popular religion of the great epics, and even the ***Vedanta*** of ***Shankara*** were conspicuous examples of tolerance in forms and ceremonies. And impressive examples of giving hospitality to Christians and Moslems are frequent in ***Hindu*** tradition. Even Buddhism was killed in India by a fraternal embrace. (Paul Arthur Schilpp, 1952: 352)

As the result of this tolerant attitude, Hinduism itself has become a mosaic of almost all the types and stages of religious aspiration and endeavour. It has adapted itself with infinite grace to every human need. Radhakrishnan is not however blind to the faults and failings of Hinduism. Indeed he tells us that it were these very faults and failings which urged him first to study its philosophy intensively. He says that I remember the cold sense of reality, the depressing feeling of defeat that crept over me, as a casual relation between the anemic Hindu religion and our political failure forced itself on my mind during those years. What is wrong with Hindu religion? How can we make it somewhat mere relevant to the intellectual climate and social environment of our time? (Lai, Basant Kumar, 1973: 353)

The tragic divergence between the exalted idea and the actual life, and the timidity in following ethics of obliging to its logical conclusion, the empty ceremonies, the superstitions, the degeneracy of the priesthood, the weakening of moral fibre, attracted his attention. Elsewhere he has written that: **Hinduism, like the creator's age, is god only in parts. It is admirable and adherent, saintly and savage, beautifully wise and**

**dangerously silly, generous beyond measure and means beyond all examples. (S. Radhakrishnan, 1975: 338)**

Yet he is convinced that ***Hinduism***, with its crude appendages discarded, in what the world needs. Hinduism requires every man to think steadily about the mystery of life until he gets the highest revelation. It insists on the development of one's intellectual conscience and sensitivity to truth. (S. Radhakrishnan, 1974: 149)

Radhakrishnan comments upon the catholicity of Hinduism that Indian culture is not radically exclusive, but has affected men of all races. It is international in feeling and intention. As the typical religion of India, ***Hinduism*** represents this spirit, the spirit that has such extraordinary vitality as to survive political and social changes. From the beginning of recorded history, Hinduism has borne witness to the snored flame of spirit which must remain forever, even while dynasties crash, expire and tumble into ruins. It alone can give our civilization a soul, and men and women a principle to live by (S. Radhakrishnan, 1947: 43)

Radhakrishnan interprets ***Hinduism*** as displaying an extreme sensitiveness to the claims of different aspects of spiritual truth. (Paul Arthur Schilpp, 1952: 371) It is an elaborate and flexible synthesis of a wide range of the cults and beliefs. And its basic scriptures may fairly be said to be universal in their significance. Commenting on the

***Gita*** he remarks that It represents not any sect of ***Hinduism*** but ***Hinduism*** as a whole, not merely ***Hinduism*** but religion as such, in its universality, without limit of time or space, embracing within its synthesis the whole gamut of the human spirit, from the crude fetishism of the savage to the creative affirmations of the saint. (S. Radhakrishnan, 1976: 12)

We may therefore conclude after Radhakrishnan that the following three points constitute the outstanding characteristics of ***Hinduism***. (Paul Arthur Schilpp, 1952: 492)

- Tolerance of all other points of view. This is not merely an experience of a superior condescending attitude that there is truth in every religion, although there is only one wholly true religion which is that of the ***Hindu***. ***Hinduism*** admits the essential truth of any religious experience in any place or time;
- The second great thing noticeable in ***Hinduism*** is its uncompromising adherence to Truth. What have been condemned are ***Pramada*** or ***"Mental Intoxication,"*** and ***Ajnana "Absence of Knowledge."*** The variety of philosophical schools within Hinduism are all something to each the same truth. Radhakrishnan therefore approvingly quotes from Mahatma Gandhi, ***"Hinduism is a relentless pursuit after truth. It is the religion of truth".*** Truth is God. Denial

of God we have known. Denial of truth has not been known. (Paul Arthur Schilpp, 1952 :492); and

- The third notable thing in Hinduism is the Principle of ***Ahimsa*** or non-injury to any life. This principle is conceived in a spirit of highest altruism and of a most enlightened and cultured negation of self. ***Ahimsa*** is not incompatible with a necessary minimum of cruelty which is inevitable in life. Just as one might uses a thorn to extract another thorn embedded in flesh. While in the negative side, ***Ahimsa*** means avoidance of injury to other living beings. On its positive side it is ***Karuna*** or ***Pity*** and ***Maitri*** or ***"Active Good-doing."***

As a religion, ***Hinduism*** contains age-old philosophic wisdom. Radhakrishnan writes, ***"There is hardly any height of spiritual insight or rational philosophy attained in the world that has not its parallel in the most stretch that lies between the early Vedic seers and the modern Naiyayikas***. (Paul Schilpp, 1952:521)

The philosophical systems with their roots in the same religious tradition represent several varieties of realism, idealism, pluralism and monism, all claiming to uphold more or less, the same spiritual tradition of the ***Upanishads***. Hinduism regards intellect as subordinate to intuition, dogma to experience, and outer expression to inward realization. Religion is not the acceptance of academic abstractions or the celebration of ceremonies, but a kind of life or experience. It is insight into the nature or reality (***Darshana***) or experience of reality (***Anubhava***). This experience is not an emotional thrill or subjective fancy, but is the response of the whole personality, the integrated self to the central reality.

It is shown by Radhakrishnan that ***Hinduism*** believes in the evolution of our knowledge of God. We have to vary continually our notion of God until we pass beyond all notions into the heart of the reality itself which our ideas endeavour to report. ***Hinduism*** does not distinguish ideas of God as true and false, adopting one particular idea as the standard for the whole human race. According to him, ***Hinduism*** accepts the obvious fact that mankind seeks God as its goal at various levels and in various directions, and feels sympathy with every stage of that search and seeking. The same God expresses itself at one stage as power, at another as personality, at a third as all comprehensive spirit, just as the same forces which put forth the green leaves also cause the crimson flowers to grow. ***Hinduism*** accepts all religious notions as facts of spiritual life and arranged them in the order of their more and less intrinsic significance. It insists on our steady spiritual progress upwards and perfecting our knowledge of God. As Radhakrishnan said the worshippers of the Absolute are the highest in rank; second to them are the worshippers of the personal God; then come the worshippers of the incarnations like ***Ramakrishna***. Buddha. Below them are those who worship ancestors, deities and sages, and lowest of all are the worshippers of the petty forces and spirits. (K. M. Munshi and R. R. Diwakar, 1969:31)

Thus he considers the relation of God in the deeper self higher than image- worship. But he provides room for the lower approaches to God and treats these with respect and understanding. (K. M. Munshi and R. R. Diwakar, 1969: 141)

The rulers of India acted up to the religious toleration principle. The theme of one of ***Ashoka's*** rock edicts says that the king, beloved of the God, honours every form of religious faith, but considers no life or honour so much as the increase of the substance of religion; whereof this is the root, to reverence one's own faith and never to revile those of others. Whoever acts differently injures his own religion while he does wrong to another. The texts of all forms of religion shall be followed under my protection. (S. Radhakrishnan, 1974)

Because of the principle of religious tolerance followed in India, the persecuted and the refugees of all great religions found shelter in India. The Jew, the Christians, the Parsees are allowed absolute freedom to develop on their own lines.

Huen Tsang reports that at the great festival of ***Prayaka*** king ***Harsha*** dedicated on the first day a statue to the Buddha, another to the sun, on the second, and to ***Shiva*** on the third. Also the famous ***Kottayam*** plates of ***Sthanuravi*** (Ninth Century A. D.) and the Cochin plates of ***Vijayaragadeva*** bear eloquent testimony to the fact that the ***Hindu*** kings not only tolerated Christianity but granted special concessions to the professor of the faith.

As Radhakrishnan says, Hinduism has adopted itself with infinite grace to every human need. It preserves unity of different beliefs by interpreting them as the difficult modes or aspects of the Supreme. This is due to the attitude which has resulted from understanding other forms of worship. Faith for a ***Hindu*** does not mean dogmatism. While full of unquestioning belief, he is at the same time devoid of harsh judgment. The ***Hindu*** attitude is based on a philosophy of life which regards religion as a matter of personal realization. Creeds and dogmas, words and symbols are only expressions of that realization.

Radhakrishnan says that ***"the Hindu religion is marked by an eminently rational character.*** ***"*** (S. Radhakrishnan, 1832: 1) Hindu thinkers have grasped the ultimate problems in a spirit, loyal to truth and feeling for reality. From the philosophical point of view, the Real is the self-identical ***Brahman*** revealing itself in all, becoming the permanent background of the world process. Religiously it is viewed as the Divine Self-consciousness, pregnant with whole course of the world, with its evolutions and involutions. The oneness of the ultimate Spirit has been the governing ideal of the Hindu religion. Even as early as the ***Rig-Veda*** the Supreme Reality is seen as one ***Ekam Sat***; therefore the learned speak of it variously. In the ***Upanishads*** the one ***Brahman*** is called by many-names according to the sphere of reality in which it is seen to manifest and function. From the epic period, the conception of ***Trimurti*** emerges and is well established by the age of ***Puranas***.

Radhakrishnan asserts that on the analogy of human consciousness, with its threefold activity of cognition, emotion and will, the view of the Supreme as ***Sat, Chit*** and ***Ananda***-reality, wisdom and joy is suggested. The three gupas, sattys or equanimity, born of wisdom, ***rajas*** or energy, which is the outcome of spirited feeling and tames or heaviness, due to lack of enlightenment and control, are the aspects that constituted all experience, and even God is not considered to be an exception to this law of the triplicity of all being. The three functions of ***Arishti*** (creation), ***Sthiti*** (maintenance) and ***Lava*** (destruction) are traced to the three gupas.

The three qualities of the one Supreme are developed into three distinct personalities. And each of the latter is said to function through its own respective ***Shakti*** or energy, and thus we have corresponding to ***Brahma, Vishnu and Shiva, Saraswati, Laxmi*** and ***Uma***, their respective ***Shaktis*** or powers. All these qualities and powers are so well balanced in the Supreme that it cannot be said to possess any quality at all. For Radhakrishnan, the one incomprehensible God who is omniscient, omnipresent and omnipotent appears to different minds in different ways.

## 2. Hinduism and Ethics

The first question that we would like to discuss in this section is: Is ethics possible in the framework of Hindu metaphysics? Can a religion which advocates the ultimate transcendence of ethics be said to be serious about ethics? At least the Christian critics of Hinduism have levelled such charges. We have now to see how the modem Hindu thinkers, especially Radhakrishnan do, reply to these charges and how they explain the ultimate transcendent of morality.

Dr. Albert Schweitzer in his Indian Thought and its Development (1936) gives clear formulation to the Christian. These charges are based on the antagonism of two world-views: ***'world and life affirmation'*** and ***'world and life negation'.*** The latter represented by Hinduism does not believe in the improvement of the conditions of life in this world. Thus ethics and life negation are contradictory to each other.

Schweitzer argues that ***Brahmanic*** mysticism had nothing to do with ethics. It inspires the individual to attain the super ethical state in liberation when identity with the Universal Soul is realized. But Radhakrishnan does not find any inconsistency between mysticism and ethics as man's realization of the fundamental unity of all existence makes him more responsive towards the other creatures on earth. He says that there is no inconsistency between mysticism and the most exalted ethics. It is a one-sided view of contemplation that makes it exclusive of moral activity. Inner perfection and outer conduct are two sides of one life. Contemplation and action, the yoga of Krishna and the ***Dhanush*** of Arjuna, are two movements merged in one act. Love is organic to spiritual life. While the eyes are lifted up to the Eternal, the arms are stretched out to embrace the whole creation (S. Radhakrishnan, 1975: 108)

Radhakrishnan does not rule out the possibility of extremists among mystics who tend to ignore human suffering in their quest for identity with Divinity. But the normal mystic never ignores his fellow creatures.

Now, ethics does presuppose a separatist view of life. Without the various distinctions between good and evil, pain and happiness, self and other, it cannot survive. So when one goes beyond these distinctions he also transcends the ethical laws. But in his temporal existence, man is in need of ethics, of dharma. Hindu thinkers were fully alive to this fact of degrees of spiritual growth. R. C. Zaehner seems to forget this when he declares:

The great defect of mysticism is that it tends to by-pass the problem of evil either by writing it off as illusory or at the most an appearance, as with ***Shankara*** or by subsuming it and 'negating' it into that all comprehensiveness which cosmic consciousness adverts Conventional religion, particularly in the Semitic tradition from which Christianity and Islam spring, takes evil very seriously indeed: the mystic, and particularly the Hindu mystic, on the other hand, tends to speak of transcending good and evil, for they are merely a pair of opposites imposed by the discursive intellect on to a fundamental unity where all the opposites coalesce and are reconciled.

Radhakrishnan refers to the doctrines of the four stages of life (***Ashramas***) including that of the householder, of Karma and rebirth as proofs for the belief in section. Buddhist ethics also advocates pity for suffering and sympathy for every form of sentient life. Thus, Radhakrishnan upholds the reverse thesis that mysticism provides a genuine cosmic foundation for human ethics that we cannot help making ourselves whether our ideals are mere private dreams of our own or bonds created by society, or even aspirational characteristics of the human species. Only a philosophy which affirms that they are rooted in the universal nature of things can give depth and fervour to moral life, courage and confidence in moral difficulties. We need to be fortified by the conviction that the service of the ideals is what the cosmic scheme demands from us, that our loyalty or disloyalty to them is a matter of the deepest moment not only to ourselves or to society, or even to the human species, but to the nature of things. If the latter is religion, then ethical humanism is acted religion. When man realizes his essential unity in his life, Mysticism and ethics, other worldliness and worldly work go together. (S. Radhakrishnan, 1976: 106)

Next, Radhakrishnan deals with the criticism that Hindu ethics puts more emphasis on inner contemplation than on outer activity. First, he contends that contemplation is not a species of inactivity; rather it belongs to a higher category of activity. It involves the ethical activity of the control of the evil passions and impulses of the individual.

Normally Hindus have lived their religious life in and through the social institutions. Some of them prefer a contemplative life in solitude to social life. But such ascetics are not confined to Hinduism only. Christianity has its fair share of ascetics. Even Dr. Schweitzer himself lived the life of a dedicated ascetic.

Radhakrishnan considers some more objections in the section ***"Some objections to Shankara's Ethics considered"*** in his Indian philosophy. (S. Radhakrishnan, 1933: 621-624).

The first objection is that there is no warrant for ethics keeping in view the metaphysical identity of the individual and the Absolute. ***"If Brahman is***

***all, there is no need for any moral endeavour."*** But Shankara does not identify the imperfect empirical level with the Absolute. And ethical distinctions relate to the empirical level and to the empirical individuals. As finite agents, individuals have to act according to ethical rules and regulations.

The second objection is that of intellectualism as Shankara considers salvation as the result of knowledge, not moral perfection. Radhakrishnan first clarifies the distinction between logical learning (***Parokaajnana***) and direction experience of Reality (***Aparoksajnana***). And the latter is not possible without moral perfection (***Cittashuddhi***). The qualities of rajas and tames have to be suppressed and the set quality has to be affirmed. This happens only by dirt of moral preparations.

The third objection is that Shankara does not ascribe ultimate value to morality. As soon as the distinction of the self from the not-self disappears, ethics becomes redundant. The moral world is the world of appearances. But for ***Shankara*** ethical action belongs to the temporal world (***Sansara***). Morality is of the nature of development. It is a means and realization is the end.

A related but fourth objection is that ***Shankara*** rejects **Karma** as unnecessary for liberation. In fact, the ***Mimamsakas*** had over emphasized the worth of ritualistic formalism and ***Shankara*** strongly denounced this overemphasis. He only points out the inconsistency between action prompted by worldly desires and liberation. But he does not reject the selfless action for general ends (***Lokasangraha***) by the liberated soul, as this kind of action does not result in bondage.

### 3. Law of Karma and Human Freedom

The Hindu Law of ***Karma*** implies that all human actions are governed by a moral law. In western science and philosophy the law of causation is capable of regulating physical causation. This law fundamentally means that moral actions lead to certain moral consequences in the near or remote future. It does not allow for any loss of the effect of work done (***Krtapranasa***). Besides, this law does not allow for any occurrence of events in an individual's life except as a result of his or her own work (***Akrtabhvuoagama***). This law explains the differences of happiness and misery, high birth and low birth, bondage and liberation from person to person. According to the modern Hindu thinkers these differences can be accounted for only by the law of ***Karma***.

But the obvious question that arises in this context is: Is this law reconcilable with human freedom and responsibility? Does this law imply predestination and fatalism? These questions have been raised by some critics of this law. The unanimous answer of the ***Hindu*** thinkers is that this law of ***Karma*** is compatible with the true sense of Human freedom.

Radhakrishnan also maintains that the theory of ***Karma*** is recognition of the rule of law not only in outward nature but also in the world of man and morals. He traces this law back to the ***Vedic*** concept of ***Rita***. This law attributes total justice to the character of God. It involves the idea that the Day of Judgment is not in some remote future, but here and now. This law absolutely clashes with the Christian concepts of divine grace and forgiveness. Radhakrishnan admits that the Hindu conception of God and His justice is different from that of Christianity on this crucial point. Of course the ***Hindu*** does not look upon prayer as a sort of Aladdin's lamp to produce anything we want. God is not a magician stopping the sun in its course and staying the bullet in its march. But His truth and constancy, His mercy and justice find their embodiment in the implacable working of the moral law. Forgiveness is not a mitigation of God's justice but only an expression of it. (S. Radhakrishnan, 1974: 53)

According to Radhakrishnan, the law of ***Karma*** also involves the rejection of the Christian concept of atonement. He says that if we deliberately fall into sin, shutting our eyes to moral and spiritual light, we may be sure that in God's world sin will find us out and our wilful blindness will land us in the ditch. A just God cannot refuse to any man that which he has earned. The past guilt cannot be wiped away by the atoning suffering of an outward substitute. Guilt cannot be transferred. It must be atoned for through the sorrow entailed by self-conquest. (S. Radhakrishnan, 1974: 53 - 54)

He also contents that the law of ***Karma*** stops at the physical and mental life of man. It does not explain his spiritual being. Even at the psycho physical level it considers only the past as determined and leaves the future to be saved by free action.

Radhakrishnan honestly observes the degeneration of the law of ***Karma*** into the fatalistic concepts of life in the medieval period of India. This law was wrongly interpreted as the excuse for the inertia and justification of escapism but Radhakrishnan strongly denies that there is any such escapist implication in the law of Karma.

## 4. The concept of *Dharma*

***"Next to the category of reality, that of dharma is the most important concept in Indian thought,"*** (S. Radhakrishnan, 1948: 52) declares Radhakrishnan. The concept will be frequently encountered in the ***Hindu*** tradition, and any genuine understanding of Hindu culture will necessarily involve considerable attention to life and thought structured around ***Dharma***. ***Dharma*** is the primary virtue in the active life of Hindus; No other term can adequately express concern for the preservation of traditional values. The ***Dharma*** appears at least fifty-six times in ***Rig-Veda*** and is found among both pre-Indian ***Aryans*** and Post-Aryan Indians (Troy Wilson Organ, 1970: 210)

The term ***Dharma*** is almost impossible to be translated into English. In some context words such as duty, morality, righteousness, justice, and benevolence seem appropriate; in other nature and truth seem to catch the meaning. The term is derived from the root ***dhr*** meaning to uphold, support, or nourish. The ***Dharma*** connotes the conserving of a thing. It is manifested in acts that preserve realities and values. ***Dharma*** is not the act. The act rjgr se is ***karma***. The concept of ***Dharma*** underlines all ceremonials, ethical, social, religious and political ideas of the Hindus. ***Dharma*** is both reality and ideality. One of the most comprehensive definitions of ***Dharma***-a definition which has the merit of including both descriptive and prescriptive aspects-is that formulated by Bhagavan Das. That which holds a thing together; makes it what it is, prevents it from breaking up and changing into something else, its characteristic function, its peculiar property, its fundamental attributes, its essential nature, - is its ***Dharma***. The law of its being primarily that which makes the world process what it is and holds all its parts together as One whole, in a beakless all binding chain of cause-and-effect, is the Law (or totality of laws) of Nature of Nature's God, ***Dharma*** in the largest sense, the world order... That scheme or code of laws, which binds together human beings in the bond of mutual rights-and-duties, of cause-and-consequences of actions arising out of their temperamental characters, in relation to each other and thus maintains society, is human law, ***Manava Dharma***. Yet again, the code of life based on ***Veda*** (all-science of the laws of nature in all her departments), the due observance of which leads to happiness here and hereafter, is ***Dharma***. Briefly, ***Dharma*** is characteristic property, scientifically duty, morally and legally religion with all its proper implications, psychologically and spiritually and righteousness and law generally; but Duty above all. (Troy Wilson Organ, 1970: 212)

The classic symbol of ***Dharma*** is the bull, whose four feet are truth (***Satya***), purity (***Sauca***), compassion (***Daya***) and charity (***Dana***). The ***Dharma*** man is the man who stands firmly in a full and happy life which culminates in self-realization and liberation. Betty Heimann isolates five meanings of ***Dharma*** centring on a concept of fixed position: (Austin B. Creel, 1977: 215)

1. Fixed position of duty;
2. Right;
3. Religious observance;
4. Secular law or one's legal status in the community; and
5. A general principle or law of nature. The underlying concept he finds to be everything which is fixed and to which an individual-is bound.

Veman Kane, in his excellent History of ***Dharmashastra*** recommends classifying the ***Dharmas*** into five groups: (Troy W. Wilson Organ: 215)

1. ***Varna Dharmas*** those having to do with the duties of classes in Hindu society;
2. ***Agrama Dharmas*** those associated with the four stages of the ideal life of a ***Hindu***;
3. ***Varnashrama Dharmas*** the rules and requirements for the life of a man of a particular class and in a particular stage of his life;
4. ***Naimittika Dharmas*** the techniques for expiating the karma, resulting from the doing of that which is forbidden; and
5. ***Sadharana Dharmas*** the duties common to all humanities.

According to Radhakrishnan the basic principle of ***Dharma*** is the realization of the dignity of the human spirit, which is the dwelling-place of the Supreme, ***"The knowledge that the Supreme Spirit dwells in the hearts of every living creatures, is the abiding root principle of all Dharma."***

The ideal of ***Dharma*** is to mark all men into realized souls. (S. Radhakrishnan, 1932 : 22) For him, the principle of ***Dharma*** refuses us to a recognition of spiritual realities act by abstention from the world, but by bringing to its life, its business (***Artha***) and its pleasures (***kama***), and the controlling power of spiritual faith. According to Radhakrishnan, when the ***Tattriya Upanishad*** asks us to practice ***Dharma*** which refers to the duties of the stage of life to which we belong. In this sense it is employed by the ***Bhagavad-Gita*** and ***Manu***. We may define ***Dharma*** for our purposes as the whole duty of man in relation to the four fold purposes of life (***Dharma, Artha, Kama*** and ***Moksha***) by members of the four groups (***Chaturavarna***) and the four stages (***Chaturashrama***). Know this to be the essence of dharma and then practice it; refrain from doing up to others what you will not have done up to yourself.

Again he says we should not do to others what will be offensive to us. This is dharma in essence: other behaviour is due to selfish desire, and: he who, by his action, mind and speech is continually engrossed in the welfare of others and who is always a friend of others, O Jajali, knows the meaning of ***Dharma***. (Religion and Society, 1947: 108)

The significance of the term "***Dharma***", for Radhakrishnan, is complex (S. Radhakrishnan, 1983: 73) It stands for all those ideals and purposes, influence and institutions that shape the character of man both as an individual and as a member of society. It is the law of right living, the observance of which occurs the double object of happiness on earth and salvation. It makes ethics and religion combined. The life of Hindu is regulated in a very detailed manner by the long life of ***Dharma***. While the spiritual perfection of man is the aim of all endeavours, the Hindu ***Dharma*** does not insist on any religious belief or form of worship. The utmost latitude is allowed in the matter of addressing and approaching the Supreme. To decide whether one is an orthodox ***Hindu*** or not, according to Radhakrishnan, is possible by seeing if one accepts or rejects the ***Dharma***! (S. Radhakrishnan 1983: 76)

***Karma Marga***, the path of action, is the application ***Dharma***-leading to the Perfection of Man, Indian and Western scholars have classified the ***Manava Dharma*** in many different ways. Some of the ***Dharma*** relates to the ordinary life of man, some to man as a seeker of emancipation, some to sex activities, and some to the tragic situations of life.

Radhakrishnan looks at ***Moksha*** or liberation as the highest ideal of man (S. Radhakrishnan, 1932: 79). For him, all men are equal as they are born of God and have to rise to the same divine destiny. Education of the individual spirit is arranged through the scheme of ashrams or stages of life and ***Varnas*** or classes of men. He also sees ***Dharma*** as one of the four values or ends of life. The traditional categories of ***Kama, Artha*** and ***Dharma*** are used in relation to the fourth end or supreme good, ***Moksha***. For him, the right regulation of our desires is also a part of ***Dharma***. So ***Kama*** or enjoyment is recognized as a valid pursuit. Since the economic needs of the community should be satisfied, if the creative impulses of men are to be liberated for the higher cultural life, we must have ***Artha*** or wealth. ***Dharma*** or duty controls the pursuit of both pleasure and profit (***Kama*** and ***Artha***).

In Hindu view of life for him, man has come into being for a divine purpose (S. Radhakrishnan, 1983: 80) He says again that it is through suffering that our weakness can be converted into strength, our ignorance into illumination. The word "***Ashrama***" comes from a root which means ***"to suffer".*** Without suffering, there is no progress; without death, no resurrection. The more we die to ourselves, the more we live to God. (S. Radhakrishnan, 1985: 81)

Radhakrishnan describes the first stage as ***Brahmachari*** or student. This stage is intended to build up the psycho-physical constitution of man. Building the body and training the mind are the principal aims of this stage. All students whether they are sons of kings or of peasants are required to beg their food. Radhakrishnan thinks that this training in poverty impresses on the mind of student that wealth is not an essential condition of good life. The second stage of ***Grahastha*** or householder begins when the student becomes responsible for a family. The last two stages of

***Vanaprastha*** and ***Sannyasa*** are meant to make an individual a servant of humanity and of God.

The ***Varnadharma*** or the ***Dharma*** of social planning from Radhakrishnan's point of view is valid at the ***Grahastha*** or householder stage. Caste system takes into account the needs of the society as well as the interests of the individual. It helps to sustain the personality of an individual for devotion to something beyond himself. According to him, caste divisions are based on individual temperament which is not immutable. (S. Radhakrishnan, 1947: 120) He thinks that in the beginning there was only one caste. We all will have either been ***Brahmins*** or ***Shudras***. (S. Radhakrishnan, 1947: 129)

Later, people are divided into different castes according to social needs and individual actions. The ***Brahmins*** are the priests and, therefore, they should have neither property nor executive power. They are the seers who constitute the conscience of society. The ***Kshatriyas*** are the administrators, whose principle is reverence for life. The ***Vaishyas*** are traders and craftsman, men of technical ability who aim at efficiency. The Shudras are the routine workers, the proletariat.

His understanding of the caste system is based on the nature of man in whom reason', 'emotion' and 'will', will be predominant. He thinks that the predominance of any of them will decide the caste of a person. These three aspects of a person correspond roughly to the three ***Gunas***. Manu mentions three principles as governing the caste of a man, viz., ***Tapas*** or individual effort, ***Shrutam*** or the cultural environment and ***yoni*** or heredity. The first is a vague test and is not available for objective use. The second depends on the home influence, which in its turn depends on the third consideration of birth. The only practicable test is birth, and this view is in consonance with the principle of rebirth and karma accepted by the Hindus. Actually, for Hinduism the essential feature is to recognize the spirit in man and in which all men are equal.

Caste as Radhakrishnan understands is diversity of function, and the goal of life is to transcend caste division by disinterested service. Radhakrishnan observes from the ***Mahabharata*** which is a sort of social adjustment which takes place in terms of caste system. Even the foreigners were admitted into the Hindu fold so long as they followed the general tradition and common law of the society. "The great empire builders, the ***Nandas***, the ***Mauryas*** and the ***Guptas***, were, according to the orthodox view, low-born. The ***Gupta*** emperors married ***Licchavis,*** who were regarded as ***Mlechchhas.*** (S. Radhakrishnan, 1947: 129)

### 5. The Sources of *Dharma*

According to Radhakrishnan, the first source of ***Dharma*** is ***Shruti*** or divine revelation which according to tradition was "seen" not composed, by the ***Rishis***. The ***Vedas***, he says, are the basis of the Hindu religion.

Though the Vedas pronounce ideals of life-practical rules and commands are found in the secondary sources, the ***Shruti*** which includes ***Dhannashastras***. ***Shruti*** literally refers to what is remembered by the sages who are well versed in the ***Veda***. Any rule in a ***Smriti*** for which a ***Vedic*** source can be found becomes invested with the authority of the Vedas. If the ***Shruti*** and ***Smriti*** conflict, the former is to be accepted. The conduct of the saint and disciplined (***Sists)*** is also a source of dharma. Local custom is also authoritative. He quotes ***Yaihavalkva*** who says that one should not practice that which, though ordained by the ***Smrit*** is condemned by the people.

Along with the conduct of the elect ***"good conscience"*** is also recognized as a source of ***Dharma***. He refers to ***Manu*** who asks us to do that which will give satisfaction to the inner self (***Antaratman***) Whatever is not so based ought to be rejected, even if it is uttered by an old man or the sage Shuka himself.[77] Radhakrishnan tells us that in the times of distress the rules of duty can be exempted. He gives an example of the sage ***Vishvamitra*** who found that it was necessary- for him to eat dog's flesh for preserving his life, and he justified it by saying that keeping alive is better than dying. One must live before one can live according to ***Dharma***. (S. Radhakrishnan, 1947: 109 - 111)

***Shruti*** is the highest authority. The ***Smriti*** or the tradition set up by human beings is second in importance. As the Vedas could not have anticipated all our situations and needs, therefore, we have to trust the wisdom of the wise that are familiar with the spirit of the ***Vedas***. They have not provided guidance for every case, but have laid down certain general principles which we may extend to new cases with discrimination and judgment.

The decision of the ***Parishada*** or assemblies of the learned can be accepted when we are convinced that they are unbiased. Cases of doubt and dispute are to be decided by them. ***Manu*** and ***Pakasaka*** laid down that a ***Parishada*** should be formed when vital changes are to be introduced in the conduct of the people. A ***Parishada*** should generally have a hundred wise ***Brahmins*** but in times of crisis, even a single individual of insight and self-control can function as a ***Parishada***. According to **Smriti Candrika,** a convention made by virtuous is as good as the authority of the ***Vedas***.

## 6. Ultimate Reality

In his approach the nature of Ultimate Reality Radhakrishnan leans upon the ***Vedantic*** concept of ***Brahman-Brahman***, the Absolute is the logical ground of everything real and existent. He conceives the Absolute as ***"pure consciousness and pure freedom and infinite possibility."*** (S. Radhakrishnan, 1971: 543) For him, the Absolute is pure consciousness because consciousness is the most ineffable and the constantly existing phenomenon. We cannot think of any kind of existence without relating it to consciousness. It is always there. It is an infinite possibility because infinite world could arise from it; this universe is only one possibility of the Absolute. It is pure - freedom because its act of actualizing a possibility is not determined by anything; it is a free act. It could have created a world different in every detail from that, which is actual. If one drama is enacted and other possible ones, one postponed, it is due to the freedom of the Absolute. (S. Radhakrishnan, 1973: 259)

Radhakrishnan is convinced that the nature of the Absolute cannot be fully comprehended through empirical categories. He says, ***"Pure 'Being' which the Absolute can is only be indicated. It can be alluded to but not described."*** (S. Radhakrishnan, 1967: 87) He also maintains that the Absolute (***Brahman***) is higher than God (***Ishwara***), the Supreme Personal Spirit. ***Ishwara*** is called the lower ***Brahman*** (***Aparabrahman***) as distinguished from the Absolute (***Brahman***) or Higher or Supreme ***Brahman*** (***Parabrahman***). In the ***Higher Brahman*** (***Parabrahman***) all is one without eternal and internal distinctions; the material world is part and parcel of Brahman, in which the material nature is transformed into the spiritual. But, for the ***Lower Brahman*** (***Aparabrahman***) the world remains as an object distinct from Him, although it does not overpower his consciousness. The ***Lower Brahman*** is a ***'He'***, not an ***'It'*** like the other. The ***lower Brahman*** continued to exist, so long as the world continues to exist. His existence depends, therefore, on the existence of the world. The world needs His guidance and control, and He exists, therefore, as Lord guiding the world. But when the whole world obtains salvation, i.e. when there is no finite spirit left that has yet to obtain salvation the world becomes one with God and the distinction between God and Absolute disappears. That, which is one without a second, without attributes or undermined and identical with the deepest self of man, is Supreme ***Brahman*** according to Radhakrishnan. We cannot, really give any adequate description of Brahman, says Radhakrishnan: for him the austerity of silence is the only way in which we can bring out inadequately our halting descriptions and imperfect standards. (S. Radhakrishnan, 1976: 20)

Radhakrishnan refers in this context to the Upanishads in which the Real is described as not this, not this (***Neti-Neti***). The ***Bhagavad-Gita*** also supports this view of the Upanishads. The supreme is said to be "***Unmanifest, unthinkable and unchanging***", ***"neither existent nor non-***

***existent"***. The Supreme is described as possessing contradictory predicates such as ***"It does not move and yet it moves. It is far away and yet it is - near."*** This indicates the inapplicability of empirical determinations to Brahman. These predicates, according to Radhakrishnan, also bring out the twofold nature of the Supreme as being and becoming. He is ***Para*** or transcendent and ***Apara*** or immanent, both within and beyond the world. The Supreme is at once the transcendent, the cosmic and the individual reality. Radhakrishnan describes Brahman in the light of the ***Bhagavad-Gita*** as the supracosmic, eternal, spaceless, timeless ***Brahman*** who - supports this cosmic manifestation on space and time. He is the Universal Spirit, ***Paramatman,*** who ***ensouls*** the cosmic forms and movements. He is the ***Parameshwarara,*** who presides over the individual souls and movements of nature and controls the cosmic becoming. He is also the ***Puruanttama***, the Supreme person, whose dual nature is manifested in the evolution of the cosmos. He fills our being, illumines our understanding and gets in motion its hidden springs. (S. Radhakrishnan, 1976: 27)

Radhakrishnan further explains the nature of Brahman as spiritual freedom or delight (Ananda), the ecstasy of fulfilled existence. Here the search of a seeker ends, not simply because his doubts are satisfied but because his doubts are stilled by the vision of self-evident Reality. He apprehends the Supreme Unity that is beyond the discursive reason and contemplates the One and is lost in ecstasy.

The ***Upanishads*** declare that Absolute Reality is ***Satvam*** (truth) ***Inanam*** (consciousness) and ***Anantam*** (***infinity***). ***Brahman*** is not merely a featureless Absolute. It is this entire world. (S. Radhakrishnan, 1953: 64) The ***Svethavatara Upanishad*** makes out that ***Brahman*** is Beast, bird and insect, the tottering old man, boy and girl. ***Brahman*** sustains cosmos and is the self of each individual. Supra-cosmic transcendence and cosmic universality are both real phases of the one Supreme. The two, ***Nirguna*** and ***Saguna Brahman,*** Absolute and God, for Radhakrishnan, are not different. Hindu thinkers, he points out, interpret the integral nature of the Supreme Reality as:

(1) The Absolute, ***Brahman;***
(2) The Creative Spirit, ***Ishwara;***
(3) The world-spirit, ***Hiranya-garbha;*** and
(4) The world

From ***Mandukva Upanishad,*** Radhakrishnan tells us that ***Brahman*** is Catue-pat, the four-footed, and its four feet are ***Brahman, Ishwara, Hiranya-garbha*** and ***Vimi.*** Again, in the ***Tattriya Upanishad,*** the Absolute is conceived as a nest from which three birds have emerged, viz. ***Viraj***, ***Hiranya-garbha*** and ***Ishwara.***

The Absolute conceived as it is in itself, or independent of creation, is called ***Brahman***. When it is thought of as having manifested itself as the universe, it is called ***Virni;*** when it is thought of as the spirit moving everywhere in the universe, it is called ***Hiranya-garbha***: when it is thought of as a personal God creating, protecting and destroying the universe, is called ***Ishwara. Ishwara*** becomes ***Brahman, Vishnu*** and ***Shiva*** when his three functions are taken separately. The real is not however a sum of these.

Radhakrishnan refers to ***Shankara*** who in his commentary on the ***Brahma Sutra*** refers to the episode: ***Bahya*** when asked by ***Baskali*** to expound the nature of ***Brahman***, kept silent. The teacher remained silent despite repeated requests of the pupil. At least the teacher said, ***"I am teaching but you do not follow."*** The self is silence. Radhakrishnan approvingly refers to the classic declaration of Plotinus: ***"We say what he is not; we cannot say what he is."*** He also compares the Absolute with the ***Sunyata*** of the Buddhists. (S. Radhakrishnan, 1953:67)

To say that the nature of Brahman cannot be defined does not mean that it has no essential nature of its own. Only we cannot define it by its accidental features, for they do not belong to its essence. There is nothing outside it. At best its ***Swarupa*** or essential nature is said to be ***'Sat'*** or ***'Being'***, ***'Chit'*** or consciousness and Ananda or bliss. These are different phrases describing the same being. Self-being, self-consciousness and self-delight are one; it is Absolute Being in which there is no non-consciousness. It is absolute bliss in which there is no suffering of negation of bliss. All suffering is due to a second, an obstacle; delight arises from the realization of something withheld, by the overcoming of obstacles, by the surpassing of the limit. It is this delight that overflows into creation.

### 7. Atman

According to Radhakrishnan, while ***Brahman*** is the eternal matrix of the universe, ***Atman*** is the fundamental reality underlying the conscious powers of the individual. He cites from ***Chhandogya Upanishad*** about this inner and true self of man that ***Prajapati*** told Indra that the ultimate self is free from sin. free from old age, free from death and grief, free from hunger and thirst, which desires nothing; imagines nothing but what it ought to imagine, that it is which we must try to understand. (S. Radhakrishnan, 1955: 74)

The self in ***Chhandogya Upanishad*** means the light of lights, and through it alone there is any light in the universe, Radhakrishnan controls this with the total depravity of the human self in John Calvin. Indian religions have discovered divinity in man, not depravity. Besides, the inherent spiritual freedom of man, he points out, is in contrast with the Calvinistic predestination theory.

For him, the self is the only abiding element of the individual. It is the final and true source of self-identity. It does not require proof; it is self proven (***Svasiddha***). Even he, who denies it, tends to assure its existence in so far as he thinks. This self though inconceivable is the ground of all conceiving and knowing. (S. Radhakrishnan, 1975:26 - 27)

## 8. Brahman and Atman

According to Radhakrishnan, the objective and the subjective, the ***Brahman*** and the ***Atman,*** the cosmic and the physical principle, are identical. ***Brahman*** is ***Atman.*** Our ***Atman,*** our inmost individual being, ***Brahman***, the inmost being of the cosmic is one.

The different conceptions of ***Brahman,*** he says, correspond to the different ideas of the ***Atman*** and vice-versa. In the early ***Upanishads Atman*** is the principle of the individual consciousness, and ***Brahman*** is the super personal ground of the cosmos. Soon the distinction diminishes and the two are identified, ***Brahman***, the first principle of the universe, is known through ***Atman,*** the inner self of man. ***Chhandogya Upanishad*** says that verily this whole world is ***Brahman***, and also ***"this soul of mine within the heart, this is Brahman." "That person who is seen in the eyes, he is Atman. That is Brahman."*** (S. Radhakrishnan, 1948: 170)

In the fourth or the truly state of the self the object and the subject become one. When we identify the ***Atman*** with the self-conscious individual, ***Brahman*** *i*s viewed as the self-conscious ***Ishwara*** with the force opposed to him. The conception of ***Ishwara*** is the highest object of the religious consciousness. When the ***Atman*** is identified with the mental and vital self of man (***Manas*** and ***Prana***) ***Brahman*** is reduced to the ***Hiranya-garbha*** or the cosmic soul, which comes between the ***Ishwara*** and the soul of men.

## 9. Doctrine of Maya

Radhakrishnan's reinterpretation of the concept of ***Maya*** is one of his greatest contributions to Indian philosophy. ***Maya*** as he interprets it is a realistic concept. It is not the same as illusion. The world is real, not an illusion. It is as real as man himself. Radhakrishnan holds that Maya only points to the phenomenal character of the world. According to him, what is not self-explanatory and yet cannot be denied as an unreality is ***Maya***. Our rational consciousness is too full of such concepts which we cannot give up and yet cannot fully explain.

He regards ***Maya*** not as illusion, but as a concept of explanation. We cannot know the why of the world, and ***"it is this fact of its inexplicable existence that is signified by the word Maya".*** (S. Radhakrishnan, 1948: 34)

Radhakrishnan, like ***Shankara***, uses the word Maya as a concept of explanation of the relation of the apparent to the real. ***Maya***, in his thought, is a statement of fact, and ***"our daily practical life in the dual world is not possible without Maya we live, move, and think in Maya inexplicable in the extreme, Maya is described as making the impossible possible".*** (S. Radhakrishnan, 1948: 170)

The ***Svetasvatara Upanishad*** describes God as ***Maya*** the wonderful working of powerful being, who creates the world by His powers. ***Maya*** is used here in the sense in which the ***Rig-Veda*** employs it. The divine art or power, by which the Divinity makes a likeness of the eternal prototypes or ideas, inherent in his nature. ***Indra*** is declared to have assumed many shapes by his ***Maya***. Again, ***Maya*** is the power of ***Ishwara*** from which the world arises. God has control of Maya; he is not subject to it. If God were subject to Maya, he would not be infinite supreme existence. Any being compelled to manifest is not free. ***Ishwara*** has in Him the power of the manifestation, non-manifestation and other-manifestation. ***Kartum arkartum, anyatha-kartum***. ***Brahman*** is logically prior to ***Ishwara*** who has the power of manifestation, and takes him over into His transcendental being when He is not manifesting His nature.

Maya also signifies ***Prakriti*** the objective principle which the personal God uses for creation.

All nature, even on the lowest, is in ceaseless movement, aspiring to the next higher stage of which it is itself an image or lower manifestation. While ***Prakriti*** is said to be the ***Maya*** of God, its forms seem to be eternal to us. It is the source of our ignorance. While the world is created by the power of ***Maya*** of ***Ishwara***, the individual soul is bound down by ***Maya*** in the sense of ***Avidya*** or ignorance.

What is the relation between the real ***Brahman*** and the unreal world for ***Shankara*** as Radhakrishnan sees, this question is illegitimate and impossible to answer. When we intuit the absolute ***Brahman,*** the question of the nature of the world and its relation to ***Brahman*** does not arise, for the truth which disarms all discussion, is seen as a fact.

Radhakrishnan interprets the relationship between ***Brahman*** and the world as non-different, so the question of the relation between the two is inadmissible. (S. Radhakrishnan, 1948: 570) The world has its basis in ***Brahman*** and the world is one and exists in reality and appearance. The finite is the infinite, hidden from our view through certain barriers. The world is ***Brahman*** since, if ***Brahman*** is known, all questions of the world disappear. These questions arise simply because the finite mind views the world of experience as reality finite forms and limits fall away. The world is ***Maya***, since it is not essential truth of the infinite reality of

***Brahman***. The term ***"Maya"*** refers to our finitude and points to the lacunas in empirical knowledge. Regarding the status of ***Maya***, Radhakrishnan comments that ***Maya*** cannot be different from ***Brahman***, which has no second. The universe is not due to any addition to ***Brahman*** from some other source or reality, for nothing can be added to that which is already perfect. It is therefore due to non-being. The process of the world due to a gradual deprivation of ***Maya*** is used as the name of the dividing force, the finessing principle, that which measures out the immeasurable central reality, neither identical with nor different from it. To give it as independent place would be to accept a fundamental realism. (S. Radhakrishnan, 1948: 570)

The moment we try to relate Maya with-***Brahman***, the latter becomes transformed into Ishwara and Maya denotes the manner affected by ***Maya***. If ***Maya*** exists, it will constitute a limit to Brahman; if it does not exist, even the appearance of the world cannot be accounted for. It is real enough to produce the world and unreal enough to constitute a limit to ***Brahman***. ***Maya*** has the two functions of concealment of the real and the projection of the unreal. The world of variety screens us from the real. Since ***Maya*** is thus deception in character, says Radhakrishnan, it is called ***Avidya*** or false knowledge. It is not mere absence of apprehension but positive error.

***Maya*** so far as it is the energy of ***Ishwara***, says Radhakrishnan, is his inherent force, by which he transforms the potential into the actual world. It transforms itself into desire (***Kama***) and determination (***Samkalpa***). As the creative power of the eternal God, it is eternal, and by means of it the supreme Lord creates even as heat in fire. ***Maya*** is identified with the names and forms which in their un-evolved condition, is inherent in ***Maya*** and in their developed state constitutes the world. In this sense it is synonymous with ***Prakriti***.

**10. Avidya**

The concept of ***Maya*** is intimately related with that of ***Avidya***. We cannot attain a perfect knowledge of reality, so long as we are subject to ***Avidya***. or the logical mode of thinking. ***Avidya*** is the fall from intuition, the mental deformity of the finite self that disintegrates the divine into a thousand different fragments.

For Deussen ***Avidya*** is ***"the innate obscuration of our knowledge,"*** the twist of the mind which makes it impossible for it to see things except through, the web of space - time - cause. The appearance of Brahman as the world is due to our ***Avidya.*** Even as the appearance of the rope, as the snake is due to defective vision. When we see the rope as it is, the snake becomes unreal. When we see the reality of world in ***Brahman***, the appearance of the world ceases to be.

There can be no real relation between the image of the snake and the reality of the rope, as no relation is possible between what is and what is not. We have only to blame the eye for the image. When we see the rope as rope, there is an end of the matter; only the rope appeared as the snake. Relativity has no cause except, defective insight.

***Avidya*** is either absence of knowledge or doubtful and erroneous knowledge. It is not simply negative; it has a positive character (***Bhavarupa***). When ***Shankara*** argues that the existence of Avidya is patent to all, he focuses on the fact of human finitude.

While ***Maya*** is cosmic in significance, ***Avidya*** is subjective. We are subject to ***Avidya*** when we look upon the multiplicity of objects and egos as final and fundamental. Such a view falsifies the truth. It is the illusion of ignorance.

**11. Maya and Avidya**

Radhakrishnan tells us that even as ***Brahman*** and ***Atman*** are one, so are ***Maya*** and ***Avidya.*** (S. Radhakrishnan, 1948: 587) The tendency of the human mind to see what is really one as if it were many, is ***Avidya***, but this is also common to all individuals.

Both ***Avidya*** of the Individual and the ***Prakriti*** of the ***Brahman***, arise together; neither of them is thinkable apart from the other. ***Avidya*** and ***Prakriti*** are co-eternal and belong to the world of experience. The space-time-cause world is the view of reality given to us through ***Avidya***. ***Avidya*** and ***Maya*** represent the subjective and the objective sides of the same fundamental fact of experience. It is called ***Avidya***. Since it is dissolvable by knowledge; but in its universal aspect it is called ***Maya*** and co-eternal with ***Ishwara***. ***Shankara*** admits its existence even on the state control over his ***Maya*** has no ***Avidya*** and if ***Shankara*** here and there lends countenance to a different view, it is to be taken in a figurative sense that ***Ishwara*** has the power which leads to ***Avidya*** in the individual.

***Shankara*** says Radhakrishnan, uses ***Avidya*** and ***Maya*** indiscriminately, but later ***Advaitins*** draw a distinction between the two. While ***Maya*** is the ***Upadhi*** or adjunct of ***Ishwara, Avidya*** is the ***Upadhi*** or adjunct of the individual.

**12. God**

Like ***Shankara,*** Radhakrishnan also maintains that God (***Ishwara***), as the Supreme Personal Spirit is lower than the Absolute (***Brahman***) God (***Ishwara***) is called the Lower ***Brahman*** (***Aparabrahman***) as distinguished from the Absolute, which is called the Higher ***Brahman*** (***Parabrahman***) as distinguished from the Absolute, which is called the Higher ***Brahman*** (***Parabrahman***). Radhakrishnan agrees with ***Shankara*** who regards Personal God as the determinate (***Saguna***) ***Brahman***. (S. Radhakrishnan, 1948: 542) Radhakrishnan elaborates the concept of ***Ishwara*** Like this, ***Ishwara*** is the supreme spirit, all knowing (***Sarvajna***), and possessed of all powers (***Aryvasktisamanvitam***). He is the soul of nature, the principle of the universe, its animating breath and actuating spring, the source and end of all existence modes (S. Radhakrishnan, 1948: 545)

He further says that ***Ishwara*** is the cause of the world. ***Ishwara*** is the first cause, since He has no origin (***Assebhava***). ***Ishwara*** as pure being (***Sanmatram***) cannot have sprung from pure being, since the relation of cause and effect cannot exist without certain superiority in the cause

***Ishwara*** is unproduced, has no cause, and is no effect. If ***Ishwara*** were an effect, then every effect from ***Akasha*** downward would be essence less and we should embrace nihilism. That which gives reality to all modifications is ***Ishwara***. ***Ishwara*** is said to be the material as well as the efficient cause of the world. (S. Radhakrishnan, 1948: 547)

***Ishwara*** combines the two principles of ***Brahman*** and ***Prakriti***. He is not pure consciousness but self-conscious personality. ***"He desired (Aiksate), I will become many I will procreate."*** Knowledge, self-consciousness and personality are possible only if there are objects.

The ***Upanishads*** declare that the universe is

in God. But they never hold that the universe is God. God is greater than the universe, which is His work. He is beyond the universe, as the human personality is beyond the body, which is the instrument of its life. From this it does not follow that God is the external Greater, existing separately from the world. God expresses Himself in the world, and the world is the expression of His life.

God is transcendent as well as immanent. The ***Upanishads*** are not pantheistic in the usual sense of the term. Things are not thrown together into a heap called God without inner unity of purpose or distinction of values. According to Radhakrishnan, philosophy of the ***Upanishads i***s against the deistic conception of God. It does not say that God is outside the world, and making. His presence is felt now and then by supernatural revelation or miraculous interference. It is pantheism, if we take it to mean to say that God is the fundamental reality of our lives, and we cannot live without Him.

Radhakrishnan describes God as every view of God from the primitive worship of nature up to the Panther-love of a St. Branois and the mother-love of a Ramakrishna represents some aspect or other of the relation of the human to the divine spirit. Each method of approach, each mode of address answers to some modes of the human mind. Not one of them gives the whole truth though each of them is partially true. God is more than the law that commands, the judge that condemns, the love that constrains, and the father to whom we owe our being, or mother with whom is bound up all that we can hope for or aspire to. (S. Radhakrishnan, 1974:22)

From Radhakrishnan's point of view, ***Hinduism*** does not distinguish ideas of God as true and false by adopting one particular idea of God as the standard for the whole of human race. (S. Radhakrishnan, 1974: 24)

It recognizes that mankind seeks God as its goal at various levels and the various directions, and so feels sympathy with every stage of the search. The same God expresses itself at one stage as power, at another as personality, at a third as all-comprehensive spirit, just as the same forces which put forth the green leaves also cause the crimson flowers to grow. We do not say that the crimson flowers are all the truth and the green leaves are false.

***Hinduism*** insists on our working steadily upwards and perfecting our knowledge of God. We have to vary continually on notions of God until we pass beyond all notions until we come to know the reality directly, which our ideas endeavour to report.

The conception of God as wisdom, love and goodness is not a mere abstract thought according to Radhakrishnan but is the concrete reality which alone can satisfy the heart of man. If we synthesize the ideas that come to us from different fields of metaphysics, moral and religion, we obtain the character of God as the primordial mind, the loving redeemer and the holy judge of the universe. The ***Hindu*** conception of God as ***Brahma, Vishnu and Shiva*** illustrates His threefold nature. ***Brahma*** is the primordial nature of God. He is the ***'home'*** of the conditions of possibility of the world, or of the 'eternal objects' in Whitehead's phrase. If the rational order of the universe reflects the mind of God, that mind is prior to the world. But the thoughts of ***Brahman*** or the primordial mind should become the things of the world. This process of transformation of ideas into the plane of space-time is a gradual one in which God is assisted by his self-creating power.

For Radhakrishnan, God pours forth the whole wealth of his love to actualize his intentions for us. (S. Radhakrishnan, 1971: 265) He takes up the burden of helping us to resist the forces of evil, error and ugliness, and transmute them into truth, beauty and goodness. The ***Rig-Veda*** says: ***"All that is bare he covers; all that is sick he cures: By his grace the blind man sees and the lame walks" "God is the refuge and friend of all."*** It further says, ***"Thou art ours and we are thine."*** God does not leave us in the wilderness to find our way back to Him.

In the light of the ***Hindu*** mythology Radhakrishnan looks upon God as an eternal beggar waiting for the opening of the door, so that he may enter into the darkness and illumine the whole of our being as with a lightning flash. It is not so much man seeking God as God seeking man. God so loves the world that he gives Himself to it. In communicating His nature to us, He makes us share in His creative power. He expects us to recognize and respond to His call and co-operate with Him. He wants us to look upon Him as our friend, lover and comrade. Therefore sin, says, Radhakrishnan, ***"consists in refusing to recognize His purpose and respond to His demand."*** Our virtue consists in assimilating the divine content and participating in His purpose. God is forever saving the world. However, Radhakrishnan tells us that God as love should not be confused with the doctrine of - predestination which may be interpreted as denial of human freedom and weakening of moral effort.

Whenever the moral order is sharply disturbed, the need for new adjustments is felt, God will manifest Himself to rescue the moral order. These special relations are called in Hindu mythology, ***Avatara*** or descents of God. The popular view holds that, whenever darkness of sin and ignorance ground the world, there is a threat to the order of the world; God Himself becomes personally incarnate in a unique way.

Radhakrishnan clears that the idea of God not only involves the values of truth and love, but also of justice. He is the perfection which rejects all evil.

For Radhakrishnan, God acts according to fixed laws. He does not break or suspend his own laws. God cannot forgive the criminal, even when he repents, for the moral order which is conceived in love and not in hatred requires that wrong doing should have its natural consequences.

Radhakrishnan insists upon the ultimate unity of the ***Hindu Trinity***: The one God created as ***Brahma***, redeems as ***Vishnu*** and judges as ***Shiva***. These represent the three stages of the plan, the process, and the perfection. (S. Radhakrishnan, 1971: 268)

So far as the world is concerned, God is organic with it. He is not detached from the world; Radhakrishnan shows this by referring to ***Rahanula***, one of the greatest Hindu theologians who regard the relation of God to the world as one of soul to body. He brings out the organic and complete dependence of the world on God. God is sustainer of the world as well as its inner guide. Struggle and growth are real in the life of God. Time is the essential form of the cosmic process including the moral life and also has a meaning to God.

According to this interpretation, life is eternal which carries us beyond the limits of temporal growth, may take us to the Absolute, but God is essentially bound up with the life in time. Progress may not be significant in relation to the Absolute, but not so in relation to God who is intensely interested in it. ***'The World Process, says Radhakrishnan, is an activity under the guidance of God, who is immanent in the process, though the goal of the process is transcendent to it.'***

The ***Hindu*** view says Radhakrishnan, maintains that the mystery of God cannot be comprehended by the mind of man. Many scriptural texts which Radhakrishnan interprets also lay stress on the inadequacy of the finite mind to understand the subtlety of God's nature. For him, God's personality is the unity of wisdom, love and goodness. His activities in relation to the world are those of action, redemption and judgment. These are represented by ***Brahma***, the cognitive aspect of God who creates; ***Vishnu***, representing God as love, redeemer; ***Shiva*** who as God omnipotent, power and perfection, judges (S. Radhakrishnan, 1985: 129) These three Gods are not three different persons but three different aspects of one God who has no second, but distinguished according to His different functions, ***Brahman*** creates us with certain potentialities. ***Vishnu*** helps us to realise them through the overcoming of opposition, and ***Shiva*** signifies the victorious self-maintenance of the Good. He is one but viewed as threefold, ***Eka eva tridha smrtah***. (S. Radhakrishnan, 1983: 132) Creation, redemption, and judgment are the three fundamental aspects of the creative evolution of the divine.

## 13. Liberation

The doctrine of liberation is a Central feature of Hinduism. In the sense it is its unique contribution to religious thought. It is inalienably related to the concept of self as pure, divine and free from birth and death and as distinct from its association with the mind and body. Out of ignorance the soul identifies itself with bodily existence and is caught up in the duality of happiness and suffering. Liberation means only the relations of the true nature of the self. With a different conception of man in a racial and historical meeting the Semitic religions have not been able to make out this conception of liberation. In Neoplatonism, gnosticism and the theory of Paul Tillich, we find only approximations of this conception.

Radhakrishnan' doctrine of liberation comes very close to that of Shankara. He believes that it is our spiritual duty to bring into play the hidden source of our being. We must get rid of the false identification with the body, life or mind. It is the uniqueness of man that in his nature seeks to transcend itself through spiritual efforts. He considers the doctrine of salvation as a distinctive feature of the eastern religions. Unlike the Semitic religions, Hinduism does not consider the plain of ethics, the body, and mind, historical progress and individualism as the ultimate destiny of man. He declares, it is a supreme status of Being in which the individual knows himself to be superior to time, to birth and death. It is not a life merely future of endless but a new mode of being, a transfigured life here and now. Rebirth is subject to time and it is inevitable so long as we stick to the individualistic position. If we transcend individualism, we rise superior to the phenomena of time and thus escape from rebirth; they are seeking us to transcend the standpoint of mere individualism and. rise to an impersonal universalism. To seek for liberation from the wheel of births and deaths is nothing more than to rise to the spiritual level from the merely ethical. The spiritual is not the extension of the ethical. (S. Radhakrishnan, 1971: 241)

The above elaboration of the concept of liberation is through and through a comparative account. The comparison is obviously but indirectly attempted here with the concept of man and his salvation in the Semitic religion. So his concept of liberation can be properly understood if we keep the Semitic views of man and eternal life.

Christianity does not consider man as a composite of self and in the Bible to the concept of ***Pefesh*** or ***Payche*** designate the whole person. The bodily being of man is not eternal, nor is it divine. He is a unit of creation like other beings and objects. His destiny does not consist in a solely spiritual world or this embodied immortality, but in the resurrection of the body; thus Christianity attaches primary importance to body in his conception of man and his destiny.

Whereas Hindu thinkers consider the transition from ethical individualism to spiritual universalism as affected by means of knowledge or ***Jnana***, the Christian tradition considers the latter as inadequate for this purpose. It considers God's grace as the only hope in fighting out ignorance. For this tradition morality is an aspect of man in his ultimate level of being. Besides, man is not considered capable of having a total vision of truth apart from its finite, historical context. Thus, men's possession of truth is confined to God's revelation to Israel and the Church in particular. Man's ultimate destiny is bound up with his moral progress in history. The Islamic view fundamentally accepts the Christian concepts of man, resurrection, hell and heaven though it does not believe on the concept of original sin. It also conceives of human life as a moral struggle. It considers social service and prayer to God as the highest expression of religious life.

The state of liberation is the end of all activity which presupposed bodily existence with the cessation of physical existence individuals cease to assist a historical being. Thus the state of liberation is a state of being not of becoming.

As we have mentioned above, the Semitic tradition believes that the historical process will never come to an end. From his perspective only individual salvation is possible but the world as a whole continues forever.

But Radhakrishnan argues for the final redemption of the world itself. He has a firm faith in a future state when the world and the individual, will march in the eternal and transcend Brahman.

**14. The Confrontation of Religions.**

From Radhakrishnan's points of view, when different systems of belief attempt to bring all people into their frames, religions discard and conflict are bound to take place because the world is only for a single absolute. (S, Radhakrishnan, 1947: 52) Radhakrishnan maintains that whenever religious life is confused with the profession and acknowledgement of certain dogmas as revealed truth, it becomes dominated by outward machinery. Such attitude coupled with the idea of supremacy of or ones religions may tend to the propagation of religion by employment of force. Any use of force will negate the spiritual value of religion. Again, Radhakrishnan points out that the hostility among religions is due to the idea of jealous god. By a fatal logic, the idea of Jealous God is supported to entail the destruction of those who worship Him under other names. (S. Radhakrishnan, 1971: 34) The more fervent the worship, the greater seems to be the tyranny of names, says Radhakrishnan. He thinks the view that God has revealed Himself exclusively to any one prophet or person and expects all others to depend on it and accept it or also to suffer spiritual destitution, is not simply a thing of the past. It works in the mind of some even now. In this sense he thinks that nothing is so hostile, and detrimental to religion as other religions, and those who have the courage to repudiate the doctrine of chosen races and special prophets and plead for a free exercise of thought about God, are still treated as outcastes.

Commenting on the attitudes of Judaism and Christianity to other religions, he writes that the Jews first invented the myth that only one religion could be true and that is their religion. They conceived themselves to be the ***'chosen people'*** of God and they had a mission to convert the whole world to their faith. (Paul Arthur Schilpp, 1952) Christianity inherited to the Judaism a passion for ethical purity and a sense of superiority. The Greeks gave way to the vague aspirations and mysteries of the spirit a logical form, a dogmatic setting. The Romans with their practical bent and love of organization helped to institutionalize religion. Thus Radhakrishnan holds that the desire for the world domination transformed the simple faith of Jesus, into an aggressively proselytizing creed. After Constantine, clerical and secular authorities, displayed systematic intolerance toward other forms of religious belief, taking shelter under the words ***"He that is not with me is against me, and he that gathereth not with me, scattereth."*** (S. Radhakrishnan, 1975:10)

Radhakrishnan points out that when Christianity was accepted by the Europeans, they accepted the Semitic creed of the ***'Jealous God'*** and the view of Christ as ***"the only begotten son of God."*** It means that Europe accepted religious intolerance which is the natural outcome of the belief in the truth once for all delivered to the saint. (S. Radhakrishnan, 1975: 324)

Coming to the religious scene in India, we find that Buddhism arose as an Indian heresy, prospered for a thousand years or so and then left to take Indian religion and culture to the rest of Asia. Christianity also appeared in the early centuries. Thus India has long been the meeting place for all the great religions.

We can say that now not only Judaism and Islam, but all other religions are our neighbours. (Geoffrey Parrinder, 1976: 22) The different religions have now come together and live together. Another is now needed most, according to Radhakrishnan is that they must develop a spirit of comprehension which will break down prejudice and misunderstanding and bind them together as varied expressions of a single truth. (Geoffrey Parrinder, 1976: 304)

## 15. Radhakrishnan on Inter-religious dialogue

Radhakrishnan is for inter-religious understanding and dialogue and suggests way to achieving religious understanding and co-operation. First of all, religion should abandon the missionary enterprise of conversation, which becomes possible when ignorance of other people's faith is removed.

For Radhakrishnan, understanding of the other religions does not mean substitution of one form of belief for another. It is to find out what others have been doing and help them to do it better.

Radhakrishnan speaks out against missionary motives, which he regards as derived from the conviction of the absolute superiority of one's own religion and contempt for other religions. These motives are akin to the political motives of imperialistic countries to impose their culture and civilization on the rest of the world. Radhakrishnan strongly criticizes missionary activities which he argues, will result in the spiritual impoverishment of the world.

He appeals to Christianity to rediscover the basic values of their own religion and live up to them. He rightly objects to Karl Barth's denial of universal revelation and voices his conviction that. We have to ***"get behind and beneath all outward churches and religions, and worship the nameless who is above every name".*** (S. Radhakrishnan, 1952:445)

According to Radhakrishnan ***'the doctrine if love'*** is common to all the major religions of the world. It is universal. To respect other religions as one respects one's own is his motto. He is against disturbing the psychological comfort of people by unsetting their faiths. Our attitudes to other religions should be in the spirit of the saying of Sophocles, ***"I was not born to share men's hatred, but their***

***love."*** The basic principles of all the great world religions are essentially meant to promoting international understanding and universal brotherhood. (Paul Arthur Schilpp, 1952: 72)

## 16. Radhakrishnan and Tolerance

Radhakrishnan asserts that the unchanging thing in the religion is the spiritual evolution of man and his awareness of the living in him. So we should take into account this basic truth above all traditions. The traditions are only imperfect, halting expressions of truth. (S. Radhakrishnan, 1952: 72) if we love truth as such and not an opinion of it or if we desire nothing except that is true and acceptable to God, the present religious snobbery and unfriendliness among religions will disappear. According to him the inter-religious discord and conflict will cease if we recognize that different religions are diverse expressions or formulations of the same truth.

In this connection he refers to ***Maitri Upanishad,*** which says. Some contemplate one name and some another. Which of these is the best? All are eminent clues to the transcendent, immortal, un-embodied ***Brahman***, these names are to be contemplated, lent and at least denied. For by them one rises higher and higher in this world, but where all comes to its end, there he attains to the unity of the person (Paul Arthur Schilpp, 1952: 72)

For Radhakrishnan, the sincere and relentless effort to understand the religions of people different from one's own is the need of the hour. He himself is an eminent example of such endeavour. (Paul Arthur Schilpp, 1952: 445) Yet we do not feel that it is all said within a simple formula.

Radhakrishnan is very much concerned about the relationship between religions of India and Christianity. He distinguishes between the early forms and later developments of the both. He contrasts the pure and simple teachings of Jesus with the developments which Christianity has undergone in the West. (S. Radhakrishnan, 1967:47)

Radhakrishnan traces the development of Christianity like this the Jews gave to Christianity an ethical passion and a sense of superiority; the Greeks gave the vague aspiration and mysteries of the spirit a logical form, a dogmatic setting; the Romans with their practical bent and love of organization helped to institutionalize the religion. (S. Radhakrishnan, 1975 : 10)

But the development of Islam, according to him, has taken the following course:

Islam is a creation of a single mind and is expressed in a single sentence. ***"There is one God and Mohammad is his prophet."*** Mohammad claims to be the final link of the great chain from Adam through Noah, Moses and Jesus...it borrows its idea of Messiah from Judaism, its dogmatism and asceticism from Christianity, its philosophy from Greece, and its mysticism from India and Alexandria. The Indian form of Islam is moulded by Hindu beliefs and practices. (S. Radhakrishnan, 1975: 339)

The faith of Jesus, says Radhakrishnan, is akin to the faith of Mohammad. But St. Paul asks us to believe in Jesus as our saviour, the very God descended into humanity. This proposition, the thinking Christians today find increasingly to status of Mohammad, is a reasonable one. I regard him as a prophet or a messenger of God, the object of whose mission was to reform the existing religion.

About Buddhism, Radhakrishnan says that Buddha did not announce a new religion. According to him, Buddha was born, grew up and died a ***Hindu***. (S. Radhakrishnan, 1983: 114)

The Buddha adopted an absolutist view of Reality, but not a theistic one. He calls himself ***Brahmabhuta***; he, who has become ***Brahman***. Thus from Radhakrishnan's points of view, Buddhism did not start as a new and independent religion. It was an offshoot of the more ancient faith of the Hindus, perhaps a schism of a heresy.

Buddha refused to acquiesce in the ***Vedic*** ceremonialism, when he was asked to perform some of the ***Vedic*** rites, he said, ***"And as for your***

***saying that for the sake of Dharma, I should carry out the sacrificial ceremonies which are customary in my family and which bring the desired fruit, I do not approve of sacrifices for, I do not care for happiness which is sought at the price of others' suffering."*** (S. Radhakrishnan, 1983: 170)

Radhakrishnan thinks that the Buddha's main object was to bring about a reformation in the religious beliefs and practices of ***Hinduism***, by making it alive to its basic principles. As Radhakrishnan says, all those who adhere to the essential framework of the ***Hindu*** religion, and endeavour to bring it into conformity with the voice of awakened conscience, are treated as ***Avataras***. So the Buddha was accepted as an ***Avatara*** who inspired Hindus to give up certain rites and practices which do not elevate man morally and spiritually and purified their religion of the numerous abuses which had crept into it. Therefore ***Puranas*** recognized the Buddha as the ninth ***Avatara*** of ***Vishnu***. (K. M. Munshi and R. R. Diwakar, 1969:449)

Radhakrishnan has an idea that the Buddha utilized the ***Hindu*** inheritance to correct some of its expressions. He has come to fulfil, but not to destroy. While the teaching of the Buddha assumed distinctive forms in countries other than India, it has become an integral part of Indian culture. The ***Brahmana*** and the ***Shramanas*** were treated alike by the Buddha and thus helped to harmonies the two. In a sense, the Buddha is a maker of modern Hinduism.

***Mahavira,*** the Twenty-Fourth ***Tirthankara*** of Jainism emphasized the relativity of religious truth and the doctrine of Ahimsa or non-violence. Buddhism and Jainism are born to fulfil a need that is felt within Hinduism. Indulgence in ritualism and rigid observance of caste restrictions despite the exalted teachings of the ***Upanishads*** prepare the way for their emergence. Mahavira and the Buddha mainly protested against such practices. They tried to purify ***Hindu*** religion and rid it of its abuses. Buddha denounced disputes about doctrines. He sits by the sacred fire of ***Brahman*** and discourses without condemning the worship, carried on there. Radhakrishnan gives an example of Siha, the general of the Licchavis who was a Jain. When he became a convert to Buddhism, the Buddha bade him to continue giving food as before to the Jains who rented his house. (K. M. Munshi and R. R. Diwakar, 1969:449)

Similarly Radhakrishnan observes that Zarathustra freed religion from the narrowness of the conception of god, the God of a chosen people, and gave an idea of god who is common to all people. He introduced purified form of worship free from blood sacrifices. ***Ahura Mazda*** (Ormuzd) is the one God, omniscient, omnipotent and omnipresent. He is the Lord of life and matter. In the cosmic process there is a struggle between two principles, the Divine and the evil. So man has to make a decision for himself and face the consequences of his choice. It is because of Zarathustra's religious reforms, says Radhakrishnan that Iran became a significant force in the evolution of world civilization.

Judaism probably took over from Zoroastrian the idea of resurrection according to which the body restored and reunited with the soul stands before God for receiving rewards of retribution for the deeds of the mortal life. Judaism and Christianity, according to Radhakrishnan are the two inheritors of the Divine will. Jesus did not completely reject Judaism. When Jesus asked his followers to go further and adopt the standards of forgiveness, of purity of love, he only broke of from the legal ideas of righteousness.

Regarding Mithraism and Christianity, Radhakrishnan says that once Mithraim swept the Roman Empire, and constituted the most formidable rival of ascent Christianity. There are many features of Mithraic mysteries which are reminiscent of the Orphic and Dionysias cults. And Christianity has more striking parallels with it, such as the idea of brotherhood, purification of baptism, birth of saviour on December 25th Sabbath asceticism and continence, last judgment, and meditating Logos. When Constantine proclaimed Christianity as the official religion of the Roman Empire, Mithraism suffered persecution and declined though it had a temporary revival under Julian the Apostate (A. D. 331-353). (K. M. Munshi and R. R. Diwakar, 1969: 458)

Radhakrishnan feels that the religious history of China and India are strikingly different from the religious history of Europe. The sectarian differences do not have the same significance in India and China as they have in the West. (S. Radhakrishnan, 1955: 40) If one is a devotee of Vishnu, it would not occur to him to look upon his neighbour who worships ***Shiva*** as a heretic', doomed to everlasting perdition. These divinities to a Hindu represent different aspects of the Supreme. Radhakrishnan refers to Chinese travellers of the early centuries of the Christian era who had left us accounts or religious life in India. According to them, Indian devotees of different sects meet together to discuss ultimate problems and of universities run by teachers of different religious persuasions. The spirit in man has one aim in all mankind; different people approach it from different sides. The presence of the Jews the Syrian Christians and Parsees in India from early times is a proof of the Indian attitude of religious tolerance.

Radhakrishnan arrives at the conclusion that people of different races, languages and cultures have met on the Indian soil and have settled down as members of a common civilization whose primary characteristics are faith in as unseen Reality of which all life is a manifestation, the primacy of spiritual experience, the relativity of rites and dogmas, a rigid adherence to intellectual norms, and an anxiety for harmonizing apparent opposites. (S. Radhakrishnan, 1955; 43)

## Chapter IV

# CONCLUSION

We now proceed to sum up Radhakrishnan's contributions to the Philosophy of religion, with a modest attempt to evaluate and appreciate the same.

Radhakrishnan's method of approach is synthetic through and through. His writings are a harmonizing force in the world of religions. Though he spent his lifetime in the exposition and neo-***Vedantic*** interpretation of Indian Philosophy and religion for the West still has primary interest, does not lie in apologetics but in a meaningful synthesis of the East and the West. C. E. M. Joad's description of him as the 'laision officer' between East and West is well suited to him.

His synthetic approach is meant to achieve harmony between the Old and New. The Old for him represents the spiritual wisdom of the ages and the New stands for the forces of rationality, science, progress, etc. His magnum opus, Indian philosophy fully reflects the ancient and medieval wisdom of India both religious and philosophical. By presenting Indian philosophy in contemporary terms to the West Radhakrishnan has done a great service to the cause of inter-religious and intercultural understanding. In spite of his learning towards ***Advaita Vedanta*** he does justice to other philosophical systems including dualists and pluralists. His interpretation of ***Maya***, of the relation between ethics and metaphysics of ***Karma*** and ***Moksha*** are his chief contributions to Indian thought. Though this is mostly a historical form of research, it is done to show its relevance to the present. Historical writing should, according to him, give us a 'feeling of the past' and 'the vibration of life', and his writings prove this.

But Radhakrishnan has cautiously avoided the pitfall of dogmatic and hero-worship. Neither does he create a halo around them nor does he neglect the uniqueness of the contemporary problems. Like existentialists he has fully taken into account the actual historical situation of each thinker of the past. Still he comes to the conclusion that the systems of Nagarjuna and Shankara are used in the western thought. This is no sweeping contention but thoroughly developed position. He could show meaningful analogies between the great thinkers of East and West.

With a profound grasp of the modern situation, especially the religious one, Radhakrishnan stresses the important value to comparative method and thinks that is most relevant to the present context of encounter between religions and cultures. Though this method is possible to present as clearly as possible the situation and spirit of every religion sympathetically. At the same time it denied finality and absoluteness to any particular religion. Radhakrishnan rightly puts emphasis on empathy and open-mindedness for understanding other faiths. He pleads not merely to brace, and patronizing pity, or condescending charity towards religions other than ones own, for genuine respect for and appreciation of them.

His basic insight regarding religion is that it is intrinsic to human nature. For him the choice is not between religion and no religion. But what kind of religion we want. This is, however a controversial issue and only a serious of phenomenological understanding of religion and its relation to human existence can throw light on the tenability or otherwise of this insight.

Radhakrishnan traces this source of religion to the awareness that life is far greater and richer than our individual Rivers can reveal. In its true sense religion means a search for truth and its realization by every individual.

It does not consist simply of dogmas and rites. He considers religion as a way of life and not merely a system of abstract ideas and doctrines. Its main purpose is to awaken man to the divine and make him realize it for himself.

He is sensitive to the distortions and degradations of the religious spirit. He points to the religious wars, persecution, inquisition, caste exploitations, etc. as instances of such distortion.

Even the hesitation on the part of religious leaders in condemning war and exploitation, constitutes religious degradation.

He rightly insists that the psychology of modern life demands a reformation of our fundamental belief. Stagnant and stereotyped religions have no relevance to this new mentality as they resist reformulation. This requires on the part of religion to emphasize, on their essential values instead of on dogmas. This shows that though Radhakrishnan is a deeply religious person, and thinker, still he is tune with the mood of his times. In this respect he is far superior to, and ahead of many contemporary religious thinkers who recourse to sophistry. Radhakrishnan has always been alive to the advances in modern science, and has attempted to accommodate science in his religious thought.

The motive behind Radhakrishnan's insistence on the necessity of religion is his insights into the nature of human civilization, its survival and growth. The essence of civilization according to him does not consist in racial unity or politics -economic organization but in the fundamental value system. And religion is the embodiment of such values. So, a civilization can attain stability and perfection through religion.

But he does not support and justify all kinds of religion. He draws a clear distinction between the Semitic religions which stress on adherence to dogmas, scriptures, ceremonies, etc. and the Indian religions which insist upon the primacy of spiritual enlightenment. The sole justification of a religion especially in the modern times -is its abilities to guide man spiritually. From this perspective the Indian religions have a greater role to play today. From the point of view of inter-religious tolerance and dialogue also he considers the Indian religions to be more valuable than the Semitic religions. The latter with the concept of the chosen people and their exclusiveness of religion contain the seeds of inter-religious antagonism. So Radhakrishnan insists that, they have to change themselves.

Religious life culminates in spiritual or mystic experience which is the foundation of all religions. This experience is higher than ritual worship of God or the Sense of awe and reverence. Besides, it gives us an insight into the nature of reality, and therefore is not a subjective or psychic state. As a true philosopher of Religion, Radhakrishnan argues with a good amount of evidence in his favour for the universality of Spiritual or mystic experience. Like Rudolf Otto, Radhakrishnan considers religious experience as unbound or undetermined by Cultural or historical forces. Such a perspective is obviously conducive to the establishment of universal brotherhood.

Mystics are 'open religion' in contrast to the creedal and ritualistic ones. The latter do provide a sense of security to weaker minds. But the former lays stress on direct communion with the Divine and thus contains the seeds of universal harmony. So the modern age plagued by discard and alienation needs the saving power of an open religion.

Hinduism is basically an open religion. ***Anubhava*** or Mystical experience is the mark of the fulfillment of life. The Buddha also stressed upon religious experience or Sambodhi. Even the systems of Hindu thought like ***Samkhya*** and Jainism which dispense with God affirm the reality of religious experience. The greatness of Hinduism lies in the fact that it gives the place of prominence to religious experience over and above rites, ceremonies, authorities and dogma. On this point Radhakrishnan has the support of most of the modern Hindu thinkers.

Radhakrishnan's strong refutation of the charge of world -negation against Hinduism is certainly praiseworthy hi this connection he points to the life of sacrifices and service (***Lokasamgraha***) by the liberated individuals as concerned in Hinduism. He also refers to the value of compassion in Buddhism of Gandhi whose Hindu religious outlook led him to social and political work.

His comparative study of Hinduism and Christianity is most extensive and also most controversial. This is one of the areas on which depends the success or failure of Radhakrishnan as a leading thinker of Comparative Religion. His insistence that in its Asiatic and Spiritualistic version, Christianity is true to the spirit of Christ, whereas its westernization is a distortion opened to debate. This shows that he had a sharp and scholarly mind .for fine distinction and the competence and sympathy to recognize the religious insights of other faiths.

Radhakrishnan tries to prove Hindu influence on Christianity through Gnosticism. The chief features of the latter are akin to those of the Upanishads. In the first century they got fused urns Jesus shows clear median influence as his religious environment included the Essences inspired by Buddhism. Therefore, Radhakrishnan claims that Jesus is closer to Hinduism and Buddhism than the Judaism. But still the tension between the two tendencies-Jewish and mystic - persisted in Christ and hence in later Christianity.

Early Christianity is humanistic, tolerant and less authoritarian. But when it became the religion of the Roman Empire it became intolerant and authoritarian. It lost its respect for other ways of religious life. This reached its climax in the Crusade wars. The protagonists of these wars forgot that the God of Christianity is the same as the God of Islam. They placed undue emphasis on the myth of the chosen people and claimed absolute finality to the Church, the Bible and the Incarnation.

As regards the fact of Incarnation,

Radhakrishnan made the vital observation that while all men incarnate the nature of God to some extent, the avatars do so to a considerable extent. Jesus was such an avatar of God. It is difficult to justify the contention that he alone had a special relationship with God which others cannot have. Though he finds it difficult to accept the doctrine of Atonement in terms of the sacrifices of Jesus he recognizes the greatness of Christianity in its idea of salvation, and its values of love and service.

Radhakrishnan adopts a twofold attitude towards Islam. Popular Islam he describes as a 'religion without mystery'. What it lacks on the metaphysical side, is more than balanced by its rational social philosophy. The rejection of the priests and rituals and its affirmation of human equality are its remarkable features. Especially he considers ***Sufism*** as akin to ***Advaita Vedanta***. He has respect for Akbar for his synthetic approach to religion. He agrees with Max Muller in considering Akbar ***'the first who ventured on a comparative study of the Philosophy of religion of the world.***'

His main, contribution to religion lies in his thesis that in the plane of mysticism alone mankind will discover its religious unity. Radhakrishnan talks of an invisible brotherhood' among the mystics. Though they are separated from each other by space and time, their religious experience revealing the spiritual identity of all, makes them members of a single fraternity. Hence the future belongs not to the organized religions but to mysticism, not to creedal dogmatism but to spiritual experience, not to any race or nation but to humanity.

Radhakrishnan's contributions to the methodology of Philosophy of Religion are also considerable. He adopted and developed certain methods of investigation with the aim of promoting inter-religious understanding and dialogue. He considers this as the need of the hour. Both in scholarship and vision, he is great among the thinkers of the modern times. The comparative method is used by him in an objective way. His conviction that truth is higher than all religions is highly significant. His appeal to the followers of all religions to discard their exclusive claims and to recognize the value of other religions is worthy of our attention. His call to different religions to cooperate in building a better civilization is gaining ground day by day.

# BIBLIOGRAPHY

1. Austin, S. Creel... 1977, Dharma
2. in Hindu Ethics, Calcutta, Firma and Private Limited.
3. Browning. Robert W., 1952, Reason and types of Institution in: The Philosophy of Sarvepalli Radhakrishnan, ed. by Paul Arthur Schilpp, New York, Tudor Publishing Company.
4. Buber, Martin, 1960, Religion as Encounter: Phenomenology of Religion, ed. by Joseph Dabney Dettis, London, SCM Press Ltd.
5. Buber, Martin, 1960, Religion as Encounter: Phenomenology of Religion, Ed by Joseph Dalney Bettis, London, SCM press Ltd.
6. Chatterji, Suniti Kumar, 1952, Dynamic Hinduism and Radhakrishnan: The Philosophy of Sarvepalli Radhakrishnan, ed. by Paul Arthur Schilpp, New York, Tudor Publishing Company.
7. Chatterji, Pritibhuchan, 1971, Calcutta, Studies in Comparative Religion. Dasgupta & Co. Private Ltd.
8. Chatterji, S.C., 1970, The Fundamental of Hinduism. Calcutta, A Philosophical Study, Calcutta University.

9. Choudary, K.P.S., 1981, Modern Indian Mysticism. Delhi, Motilal Banarsidas.

10. Creel, Austin B., 1977, Dharma in Hindi Ethics, Calcutta, Firma KLM Private Limited.

11. Das, Bhargva, 1960, Essential Unity of All Religion. Bombay, Bharatiya Vidya Bhavan.

12. Datta, Bhirendra Mohan, 1970, The Chief Currents of Contemporary Philosophy. Calcutta, The University of Calcutta.

13. Hick, John, 1975, Philosophy of Religion. New Jersey, Prentice Hall.

14. Hyde, Lawrence, 1952, Radhakrishnan's contribution to universal Religion, "'The Philosophy of Sarvepalli Radhakrishnan. ed. by Paul Arthur Schilpp, New York, Tudor Publication Company.

15. Lai, Basant Kumar, 1973, Contemporary Indian Philosophy, Delhi, Motilal Banarsidas.

16. Narvane, V. S., 1964, Modern Indian Thought Bombay, Asia Publishing House.

17. Organ, Troy Wilson. 1979, The Hindu Quest for the Perfection of Man, Ohio, Ohio University.

18. Otto, Rudolf, 1959, The Idea of the Holy. Tr. John W. Harvey, Penguin Books.

19. Radhakrishnan. S., 1951, Religion and World Unity: The Hibbert Journal. April 1951.

20. Radhakrishnan, S., 1971, An Idealist View of Life. Bombay, George Allen & Unwin (India) Private Limited.

21. Radhakrishnan, S., 1967, East and West in Religion. London, George Allen & Unwin Ltd.

22. Radhakrishnan, S., 1955, East and West Some Reflections. Beatty Memorial Lectures, first series, London, George Allen & Unwin Ltd. Radhakrishnan, S., 1975, Eastern Religions and Western Thought Delhi, Oxford University Press.

23. Radhakrishnan, S, 1940, Gautama the Buddha. Bombay, Hind Citable Ltd., Publishers.

24. Radhakrishnan, S., 1948, Indian Philosophy. Vol I& Vol II. London, George Allen & Unwin Ltd.

25. Radhakrishnan, S., 1983, Indian Religions. Delhi, Orient Paperbacks.

26. Radhakrishnan, S., 1929, Kaki or the Future of Civilization. London, Trench, Trubuor and Co., Ltd.

27. Radhakrishnan, S., 1967, Recovery of Faith. Delhi Orient Paperbacks.

28. Radhakrishnan, S., 1968, Religion and Culture. Delhi, Orient Paperbacks.

29. Radhakrishnan, S., 1947, Religion and Society. London, George Allen and Unwin.

30. Radhakrishnan, S., 1967, Religion in Changing World. London, George Allen and Unwin.

31. Radhakrishnan, S., 1962, Living with a purpose. Delhi, Orient Paperbacks.

32. Radhakrishnan, S., 1976, The Bhagavad-Gita. Bombay, Blackie and Son (India).

33. Radhakrishnan, S., 1960, The Brahma sutra. The Philosophy of Spiritual Life. London, George Allen & Unwin Ltd.

34. Radhakrishnan, S., 1932, The Heart of Hindustan. Madras, G.A. Hatoca & Co.

35. Radhakrishnan, S., 1974, The Hindu View of Life. London. George Allen & Unwin Ltd.

36. Radhakrishnan, S., 1970, The Present Crisis of Faith. Delhi, Orient Paperbacks.

37. Radhakrishnan, S., 1953, The Principal Upanishads. London, George Allen & Unwin Ltd.

38. Radhakrishnan, S., 1936, The Religion We Need. Earnest Benn Limited, Bouvoric House!

39. Radhakrishnan, S., 1978, The Spirit of Religion, Bombay, Hind Pocket Books.

40. Radhakrishnan, S., 1980, Towards a New World. New Delhi, Vision Books.

41. Reyna, Ruth, 1962, The Concept of Maya from the Vedas to the 20th Century. Bombay, Asia Publishing House.

42. Smith, Huston, 1958, The Religion of Man, New York, Harper & Row.

43. Smith, W. G., 1978, Religious Diversity. New York, Harper and Row.

44. Smith, Wilfred Cantwill, 1978, The Meaning and End of Religion. San Francisco, Harper & Row Publishers.

45. Spencer, Sydney, 1966, Mysticism in Religion. London, George Allen & Unwin Ltd.

46. Wach, Joachim, 1952, Radhakrishnan and the Comparative Study of Religion: The Philosophy of Sarvepalli Radhakrishnan. ed. by Paul Arthur Schilpp, New York, Tudor Publishing Company.

❖❖❖